THE DREADFUL
FRAUDS

THE DREADFUL FRAUDS

CRITICAL RACE THEORY AND IDENTITY POLITICS

Philip Leigh

Produced in the Republic of South Carolina by

SHOTWELL PUBLISHING LLC

Post Office Box 2592

Columbia, So. Carolina 29202

www.ShotwellPublishing.com

Cover: Adapted from U.S. Air Force photo courtesy of Wikimedia Commons

ISBN: 978-1-947660-62-5

10 9 8 7 6 5 4 3 2 1

TABLE OF CONTENTS

PREFACE...vii

CHAPTER ONE: 1
CLEAR AND PRESENT DANGER

CHAPTER TWO: 19
CRITICAL RACE THEORY

CHAPTER THREE: 35
RADICAL FEMINISM

CHAPTER FOUR:..49
CORRUPTED MILITARY

CHAPTER FIVE: 61
BIG TECH

CHAPTER SIX: 71
ANTIRACISM

CHAPTER SEVEN: 83
REWRITING REALITY

CONCLUSION 99

BIBLIOGRAPHY 101

PREFACE

IN 2015 DYLANN ROOF was a twenty-one-year-old white South Carolina loner. Even though not a member of any racist group he had indoctrinated himself online into becoming a white supremacist. One day he resolved to start a race war by killing multiple blacks. He entered a black church in Charleston where he murdered nine members and injured one with a semi-automatic pistol. After the police captured him, they discovered he owned a jacket decorated with miniature apartheid era flags for Rhodesia and South Africa. He also had photos of himself holding a souvenir replica of a Confederate battle flag and a burning American flag. Although the Confederate flag was also popular among many law-abiding South Carolinians as a symbol of their family and state heritage, then-governor Nikki Haley led a successful drive to get the flag removed from the state capitol grounds.

Thereafter, hundred-year-old Confederate statues increasingly started coming down. Most were cenotaphs to the common soldiers who had fallen on far away fields. Statue critics generally did not realize that comparatively few Confederates owned slaves. According to historian William C. Davis, "Probably 90% of the men who wore gray had never owned a slave and had no personal interest at all either in slavery or the shadow issue of states' rights. The widespread Northern myth that the Confederates went to the battlefield to perpetuate slavery is just that, a myth. Their letters and diaries, in the tens of thousands, reveal again and again that they fought and died because their Southern homeland was invaded, and their natural instinct was to protect home and hearth."[1]

---

1 William C. Davis, *The Cause Lost*, (Lawrence: Kansas University Press, 1996), 183

But the politicians and mobs didn't care. Local politicians wanted population growth. If Confederate icons suggested racism to newcomers, they would remove the memorials. The mobs and social elites were more like bullies determined to impose cultural genocide on the South. After the statue destruction mobs gained practical immunity from laws protecting the memorials in the summer of 2020 due to public temper tantrums in the wake of mostly dubious claims about racial police brutality, I responded with *Causes of the Civil War*, my previous book.

Its purpose was to help rehabilitate Confederate iconography by showing that Northerners did not go to war to end slavery and that their common refrain of wanting to "preserve the Union" had a different meaning in the South. Where the North saw "preservation" by forcing the seceded states back into the Union, the South saw "coercion." That irreconcilable difference in perspective is why the war happened because the North could have let the South leave peacefully if Northerners truly wanted to be rid of slavery.

Since disdain for Confederate Memory continued to grow, I concluded that a force beyond historical distortions about the Civil War was at work. For many years public polls showed that most Americans believed the statues symbolized Southern Heritage, not racism. In 2017 the American Battlefield Trust surveyed subscribers to their *Hallowed Ground* magazine and learned that 97% wanted Confederate statutes to remain on National Battlefield Parks. Almost 85% did not want Confederate monuments removed from other locations. Over 90% endorsed a statement that Robert E. Lee is "worthy of respect today" whereas only 9% endorsed a statement that Lee is unworthy "of respect in society today."

Significantly, two-thirds of the respondents descended from Union soldiers and only 22% were from the former Confederate states. Nevertheless, the Trust virtually ignored the survey results. Pragmatically speaking, they censored them and have ever since encouraged the removal of Confederate icons by their acquiescence, even to mob action.

By early 2021 it was evident that the Trust had been swept up by Identity Politics along with the rest of America's elite. By uniting with Critical Gender Theorists (i.e., radical feminists), Critical Race Theory (CRT) proponents have been trying to fundamentally transform our country. Both teach that America is divided into two factions: oppressors and victims. In terms of race, the oppressors are whites. In terms of gender, the oppressors are males.

Both are wrong. Barack Obama's two presidential terms and the long line of black immigrants trying to get into our country show that American systemic racism is minimal. Similarly, while females have abundant affirmative action programs compared to almost none for men, the fact that 60% of college students are female shows that women are not a disadvantaged minority, but a favored majority.

Since blacks compose 13% of America's population and women over 50%, a coalition of feminists and CRT followers could gain control of America. Both seek remedies for their alleged oppression through quotas. They eschew equality of opportunity for the individual and instead seek equality of outcome for each gender, racial and ethnic group. Sheryl Sandberg, Facebook's number two executive, believes "job openings should be contested by equal numbers of women and men." Ibram Kendi, a leading spokesman for CRT correctives argues, "The only remedy to past discrimination is present discrimination. The only remedy to present discrimination is future discrimination."[2]

In combination, CRT and feminism have morphed into a concept of identity-based victimhood determined by one's immutable characteristics such as skin color and sex. The philosophy puts white males at the top of the oppressor class. Any denial by them that they are neither racist nor misogynistic is taken as proof that they are unaware of their prejudices. Therefore, the so-called oppressors are increasingly subjected to institutionally mandated "conversations" about race and sex to discover their inner biases.

In truth, the "conversations" are merely one-way indoctrinations. Participants are taught that meritocracies are wrong; that they must step aside to make room for ethnic minorities and women. Such teachings are not limited to adults. Due to the dominance of feminists in the teachers' unions, identity-based privilege and victimhood is taught in many K-12 schools. Young white boys are taught that their natural competitiveness is a poisonous trait of traditional masculinity.

---

2 Ibram Kendi, *How to Be an Antiracist*, (New York, One World, 2019), 19; Robert Booth, "Sheryl Sandberg Calls for Policy Changes," *The Guardian*, (July 30, 2017): https://tinyurl.com/2p9yzeb7

Conversely young blacks are taught that they are needy victims entitled to riot and loot under the shield of "no justice, no peace" chants. A 2021 Yale University survey revealed that 35% of students first learned about Critical Race Theory in high school.[3]

Ultimately, CRT teaches whites they are inherently racist. Conversely, it teaches blacks they are victims so long as blacks collectively don't have parity with whites by numerous group metrics such as wealth, income, and education, among others. Blacks are further taught that they are entitled to deliberate racial preferences despite fifty-five years of affirmative action and $22 trillion in more than eighty means-tested welfare programs since the start of The War of Poverty in 1964. Until then, they cannot be held responsible for collective underperformance based upon behavior, an allegation that CRT teaches is deeply racist.[4]

Critical Race Theory and Identity Victimhood are enemies of America's traditional virtues. This book is intended to disclose the fraud and help defeat it.

---

3 Jim McLaughlin and Rob Schmidt, "National Undergraduate Study: Executive Summary," *McLaughlin & Associates*, 6-7, (September 28, 2021)

4 Heather MacDonald, *The War on Cops,* (New York: Encounter Books, 2016), 49

CHAPTER ONE:

CLEAR AND PRESENT DANGER

CRITICAL THEORY is a clear and present danger to America's survival. As a derivative of nineteenth century Marxist Theory, it seeks to achieve an unattainable equality of group outcomes at the expense of an individual's freedom to determine his own future. It replaces individual equality of opportunity with a totalitarian rule to futilely strive for a collective equality. It contends that our society is the product of a contest between conflicting victim and oppressor factions.

In terms of Critical *Race* Theory (CRT), whites are deemed the oppressors, perpetually victimizing minority races, particularly blacks, who are the oppressed. When North Dakota banned CRT in late 2021 it provided a good one sentence definition: "Critical Race Theory [is] the theory that racism is not merely the product of individual bias or prejudice, but that racism is systemically embedded in American society and the American legal system to facilitate racial inequality." As for Critical *Gender* Theory, commonly known as feminism, women are deemed the victims and men the oppressors.

All Critical Theories subscribe to the most cynical interpretations of Western and American history. They deliberately search for the most shameful aspects of our past and use those as the yardsticks to measure our morality. Feminists, for example, misinterpret the male's traditional role as the family breadwinner to be an intentional effort to restrict women's freedom. They are blind to its purpose for enabling women to civilize society through child rearing and homemaking. In the nineteenth century the size of Mrs. William Astor's ballroom was the determining factor that defined New York's elite society to its legendary 400 members.

Similarly, many Critical Race Theorists believe that our 1776 Revolution was planned to protect American slavery as opposed to creating a constitutional republic designed to limit the power of a

1

distant central government. But it is the latter that induced France to give us the Statue of Liberty in 1884. Lady Liberty still entices others to immigrate, including many racial minorities who come illegally despite our alleged systemic racism.

In principle there's nothing wrong with teaching Critical Theory as a college course that explores one possible explanation of how America's racism might have evolved. But that is not what is happening. Only in college is it sometimes taught as a theory. In the pre-college public schools, it is taught as fact to the teachers. Consequently, their teachings focus is on the alleged remedies to an accepted theory without any testing of the theory's validity. Chief among such remedies is so-called antiracism. Among the leading antiracist apostles is Ibram X. Kendi, a black humanities professor at Boston University. According to Kendi, nobody can simply be "not racist." One can only be "racist" or "antiracist." Anyone who does not support antiracism is a racist. Put another way, there is only Us and Them. Disagree with Us and you're racist, even if you don't realize it. That's Kendi's Catch 22 for whites. If you confess that you're racist you've admitted your unforgivable sin. If you fail to confess your sin, your very denial is proof of your unpardonable guilt.[1]

A September 2021 survey of undergraduates commissioned by the William F. Buckley, Jr., Program at Yale disclosed revealing opinions about race among college-age people. By a 49% to 42% margin, they believe that America is inextricably linked to white supremacy and has not fulfilled its promise for black equality implied in the Declaration of Independence. Consequently, two-thirds of students believe that most Americans need to be re-educated about our racial history. Nearly 60% favor the teaching of Critical Race Theory, twice as many as oppose it.

By sex, male students believe America is moving forward by a 53% to 40% margin whereas females disagree by a 56% to 35% margin. The women lament that our country remains linked to white supremacy. Almost 40% think that America should try to correct for past racial injustices by paying reparations to the descendants of former slaves or by some other redistribution of wealth along racial lines. Over 70%

---

1 Ibram Kendi, *How to Be an Antiracist*, 9, 19-20, 64; David Horowitz, *The Enemy Within*, (Washington, D. C.: Regnery Publishing, 2021), 157

believe that "systemic racism" is a big problem. Liberal students agree by a 90% to 10% margin whereas conservatives are almost evenly divided with a 51% to 49% margin.[2]

In terms of race, Kendi defines an antiracist as anyone who supports policies that reduce the disparities between blacks and whites collectively. Discrimination is okay if it weakens the oppressors and uplifts the oppressed. "To be an antiracist is to view the inequities between all racialized ethnic groups as a problem of policy...The defining question is whether the discrimination is creating equity or inequity. If it is creating equity, then it is antiracist. If the discrimination is creating inequity, then it is racist." Thus, he concludes, "The only remedy to racist discrimination is antiracist discrimination. The only remedy to past discrimination is present discrimination. The only remedy to present discrimination is future discrimination." But the last quote presents at least two problems.

First, it would hold America in a perpetual state of anti-white discrimination until blacks and whites collectively achieve equal outcomes, such as per capita income or wealth. Left unanswered is the question of who is to determine when the groups are equal. If it can be measured fairly, Critical Race Theory implies that when at parity blacks will be at the threshold of themselves becoming the oppressor race due to lingering racial preferences. Assuming anti-white discrimination leads blacks to become equal in education should the policy continue until it over-corrects thereby transforming blacks into the oppressor class and whites into the victims? If the reader does not think that could happen, consider that feminists continue to promote affirmative action for females, notwithstanding women presently are 60% of college students and have been a majority for decades.

According to the *Wall Street Journal*, "American colleges, which are embroiled in debates over racial and gender equality, ... have yet to reach a consensus on what might slow the retreat of men from higher education. Some schools are quietly trying programs to enroll more men, but there is scant campus support for spending resources to boost male attendance and retention." Even though the Pell institute reports

---

2 Jim McLaughlin and Rob Schmidt, "National Undergraduate Study: Executive Summary," *McLaughlin & Associates*, 6-7, (September 28, 2021)

that poor and working-class white men enroll at lower rates than those of black, Latino and Asian men from the same economic background, white males are immutably categorized as oppressors on campus.[3]

Second, even if his antiracist "remedy" is accepted, Kendi fails to realize that there are likely to be irreconcilable differences over the policy specifics. His book provides only a limited antiracist definition: "Antiracism is a powerful collection of policies that lead to racial equity [collectively] ..." Affirmative action is among such policies. But affirmative action has been in place for fifty-five years and black students still cluster toward the bottom of class rankings. When Kendi entered the third grade in 1990, he writes, "Asian fourth graders scored thirty-seven points, Whites thirty-two points, and Latinx twenty-one points higher than Black fourth graders on the standardized math test. By 2017, the scoring gaps in fourth grade mathematics had [only] slightly narrowed."[4]

Consequently, some people of good faith argue that affirmative action should be abandoned in order to *benefit* of blacks. Among them is Hoover Institution Fellow Shelby Steele, the son of a black father and white mother. In Steele's analysis, decades of habitual race preferences have caused blacks to regard them as entitlements, tempting recipients to evade personal responsibility. Agreeing with Steele is Brown University's Economics Professor Glen Loury, who also is black: "[Unlike in the 1960s] this is a level playing field we're dealing with here in 2021. America is the freest, most dynamic, most prosperous society that millions of people are willing to risk everything just to get into. We [African Americans] are birthright citizens here. The ball is in our court." White analyst David Horowitz postulates a Mismatch Theory, suggesting that affirmative action perpetuates inequality because it puts racial minorities in situations where they are likely to fail since they can't keep up with their better prepared white peers.

According to Heather MacDonald's *Diversity Delusion*, blacks enter Duke University with average Scholastic Aptitude Test (SAT) scores of 1280 as compared to 1420 for whites and 1460 for Asians. Although black grades are significantly below those of whites and

---

3 Douglas Belkin, "American Men Give Up On College, 'I Just Feel Lost,'" *The Wall Street Journal,* (September 6, 2021): https://tinyurl.com/2p9abxa3
4 Ibram Kendi, *How to Be an Antiracist*, 9, 19-20, 99

Asians during the first year, by the fourth year the difference is narrowed to half. But the improvement is illusionary because many blacks change their majors. They switch out of the demanding science and economics programs into the humanities where the courses are easier. If black freshman did not switch majors, the grades between blacks and whites would not converge.

Significantly, Duke's black freshmen get higher grades in the humanities and social sciences than do freshmen of all races in the hard sciences even though the blacks have significantly lower aptitude test scores. The students themselves report that the explanation lies with the lower humanities coursework demands. Students majoring in the hard sciences report spending 50% more time studying science courses and rate them harder than humanities and social science classes.

One statistical study MacDonald cited examined the completion differences between Duke's black and white hard science majors. More than three-fourths of black male freshmen intended to major in the hard sciences, an even larger share than white male freshmen. But more than half of the would-be black science majors switched track compared to less than one tenth of the white males. In the fourth year, 63% of the white male cohorts graduated with diplomas in the hard sciences as compared to only 35% of blacks. Black attrition from the science programs was entirely due to their lack of academic preparedness relative to whites; race was irrelevant.[5]

Alternately, affirmative action has left conscientious and well qualified blacks vulnerable to "imposter syndrome." One consequence of affirmative action is that beneficiaries may be perceived as undeserving; that their academic and career accomplishments result from racial preferences and tokenism, suggesting that their true abilities are lower than their white classmates. When they internalize the perception, they fall prey to "imposter syndrome." They self-discredit their determination and skills, tending to think of themselves as phonies whose success is due to affirmative action and quotas.

---

5 Shelby Steele, *White Guilt*, (New York: Harper Perennial, 2006), 37, 152, 174; Heather MacDonald, *The Diversity Delusion*, (New York: St. Martin's Press, 2018), 53-4, 56; Glenn Loury, *Hoover Institution Interview*, (November 22, 2021): https://tinyurl.com/mr2t5scv

Black Supreme Court Justice Clarence Thomas is particularly sensitive on the point. After he arrived from Savannah at Holy Cross College near Boston in 1968, he came to sense Northern racism was more virulent than the Southern version. Three years later he enrolled at Yale Law School under an affirmative action program. "As much as it had stung to be told I'd done well in [high school] despite my race," he later wrote, "it was far worse to feel that I was now at Yale because of it."

One of his favorite songs while at Yale was "Smiling Faces Sometimes." The lyric—"Smiling faces tell lies"—underscored his experience with Northern white liberals. He came to believe that they offered help to blacks to express the privileges of race and class. As a result, the belief that blacks can only advance with the help of whites is anathema to Thomas. Such vouchsafed benevolence denies blacks the pride of achievement. Thomas has long opposed affirmative action for that very reason. He takes it as a form of reverse racism, which illegitimately burdens whites. Yet he also perceives that white liberals use affirmative action to brand blacks as inferior.

His argument stems from two tenets. First, affirmative action stigmatizes blacks because whites commonly believe that "blackness" signifies intellectual inferiority, much like a hillbilly accent among whites. He once opined that even Supreme Court Justices "assume that anything that is predominantly black must be inferior." When institutions identify blacks as needing help, they reinforce the stigma. Second, affirmative action perpetuates white supremacy by portraying whites as virtuous benefactors willing to disadvantage the lower-class members of their own race for the sake of appearances. Chelsea Clinton, for example, breezed into Stanford, NBC, and McKinsey & Company but it is doubtful that any whites from her Little Rock public grade school hopped on a similar track.[6]

More concretely, while Kendi might think that affirmative action is a good antiracist policy to increase the number of blacks at top universities, there may be better ideas that he would likely reject. One probable example is the outlawing of public sector labor unions. Labor contracts won by teachers' unions often make it nearly impossible to

---

6 Theodore Johnson, "A Missed Opportunity in Racial Preferences," *The Wall Street Journal*, (June 24, 2013); Corey Robin, "Clarence Thomas's Radical Vision of Race," *The New Yorker*, (September 19, 2019)

dismiss incompetent teachers. Even though charter schools are heresies to such unions they more often improve black student performance and get more of them into the top colleges. Surely, such schools should be given a chance after nearly six decades of affirmative action failure.

Despite his emphasis on the collective, Kendi's parents showed him the value of personal responsibility by example. Both had successful careers. They were deeply involved in Ibram's school choices and believed that widespread personal irresponsibility was the chief factor holding other black families back. Perhaps his rejection of their wisdom is a form of unresolved teenage rebellion.[7]

Notwithstanding nearly universal endorsement among academics, differences among black ethnic groups themselves suggest that racial preference programs are counterproductive. Although blacks in the United States have a median income of $41,500, the amount for Nigerian immigrants is $52,000. Nearly 30% of Nigerian Americans have college degrees compared to 11% for all Americans. They account for about 1% of all black Americans but compose almost 25% of the blacks attending Harvard Business School. Such performance is consistent with a native Nigerian axiom: "The best inheritance that a parent can give to their children is not jewelry nor any other material things, but a good education." A 2016 paper by Cynthia Hudley in the *International Journal of Educational Psychology* shows that black U.S. immigrants from both Africa and the Caribbean do better economically and academically than African Americans.

During his youth Kendi discovered first-hand that black immigrants perform better than African Americans. Citing interviews conducted by researcher Mary C. Waters he later learned that Caribbean black immigrants regarded African Americans as "lazy, unambitious, uneducated, unfriendly, welfare dependent, and lacking in family values." But rather than see any legitimacy in such points, his personal attitude echoed Waters' interviews with African Americans who categorized Caribbean blacks as "selfish, lacking a race awareness, being lackies to whites, and [having] a sense of inflated superiority." Instead of discerning how he might benefit from emulating the Nigerian and Caribbean students, Ibram hunted for ways to discredit them.

---

7 Ibram Kendi, *How to Be an Antiracist*, 27

When he was teaching at the State University of New York in Albany, he entered a dialog with a black Ghanaian student. During an earlier class the student spoke out about his perception of African Americans. It was a near perfect copy of the criticisms that interviewer Waters had recorded regarding welfare dependency, laziness, and so on. Kendi's response was to use his superior status as the teacher to brainwash the student. Kendi convinced the young man that his criticisms of African Americans were racist. But to soften the accusation he added that the African Americans were also racist toward him when they regarded Caribbean blacks as selfish, smugly superior, and unaware racially. Kendi claimed that the Ghanaian and African American were being racist toward one another.

That argument is based on "cultural relativism," a term that holds cultures to be merely different without one being better than the other. But that is not necessarily true. In fact, it is sometimes seriously wrong. Let Kendi ponder, for example, whether a culture that endorses slavery is superior to, or merely different from, one that does not.

Similarly, a "selfish" student devoted to studying while his classmates play, may be more likely to succeed than one who relies upon welfare to get by. Likewise, a two-parent family that values personal responsibility and eschews welfare probably provides a better success setting than does a single parent welfare-dependent one. In fact, single parenthood is itself often an irresponsible act. Since 64% of African American families are single parent households as compared to 24% of whites, perhaps the Ghanaian student should imitate white behavior. If it yields him a better education than his welfare-dependent classmates, he should be ashamed when they jealously deride him.[8]

In August 2021 University of Chicago Geophysicist Dorian Abbot penned a *Newsweek* Op-Ed opposing affirmative action and identifying often overlooked consequences. "Viewed objectively, American

---

8 Ibram Kendi, *How to Be an Antiracist*, 61, 63-66; Philip Salzman, "False Justification for Anti-Racism," *Epoch Times*, (September 8, 2021); Cynthia Hudley, "Achievement and Expectations of Immigrant, Second Generation and Non-Immigrant Black Student in U. S. Higher Education," *International Journal of Educational Psychology*, (October 24, 2016): https://tinyurl.com/yckk4krn; B. Joseph, "Why Nigerian Americans are One of the Most Successful Ethnic Groups in the U.S.," *Medium*, (July 2, 2018): https://tinyurl.com/yc5ejse4

universities are already incredibly diverse. They feature people from all countries, races, and ethnicities. This is in stark contrast with most universities in Europe, Asia, and South America. American universities are not diverse because of DEI (diversity, equity, and inclusion), but because they have been extremely competitive at attracting talent from all over the World. Ninety years ago, Germany had the best universities. Then a race-obsessed regime came to power and drove many of the best scholars out, gutting the faculties and leading to a sustained decay that German universities never recovered from."[9]

When Professor Phoebe Cohen at Williams College learned that Dr. Abbot had been invited to make a geophysics presentation for a prestigious lecture series at nearby Massachusetts Institute of Technology (MIT,) she complained. Even though Cohen had no current connection to MIT, the *New York Times* amplified her complaint. Consequently, MIT rescinded Abbot's invitation after the *Times* article disclosed that he had written the *Newsweek* Op-Ed opposing affirmative action.

Nonetheless, the *Times* reporter asked Cohen whether silencing Abbot was a better option than allowing affirmative action to be debated in the spirit of academic truth-seeking. Cohen responded, "This idea of intellectual debate and rigor as the pinnacle of intellectualism comes from a World in which white men dominated." Evidently without realizing it, she is asserting that minorities and women do not have the intellectual capacity to compete on a level playing field with white males. No doubt, many successful women, if not feminists, feel she is underestimating their abilities.[10]

Since the mid-1960s most American whites have progressively sought ways to disassociate themselves from racism. Initially they focused on historical racism but have increasingly wanted to disconnect from today's alleged systemic racism. Presently people on the political Left cannot pass up any opportunity to disassociate themselves as a virtue signaling exercise. That's because "whiteness" has become distorted into a symbol of evil over the past sixty years.

---

9 Dorian Abbot and Ivan Marinovic, "The Diversity Problem on Campus," *Newsweek,* (August 12, 2021)

10 Rod Dreher, "Professor: Intellectual Rigor is Racist," *The American Conservative,* (October 20, 2021).

In the World of Identity Politics, whites lost even a basic right to white identity. Anglo-Saxon descendants cannot celebrate their ancestors' achievements without being deemed as having aligned themselves with white supremacy. They cannot even celebrate their patriotism, which the "woke" community suspects is a dog whistle for white nationalism. To disassociate themselves from such judgements, many whites sacrificed Confederate statues, or any historical Anglo-Saxon figure, supposedly connected to past racial norms.

To gain employment in Corporate America, or admission into top colleges, today's whites must demonstrate contrition and deference by pledging allegiance to diversity, equity, and inclusion. As shall be discussed, no white can go far even in the military without genuflecting to diversity. Beyond an identity that apologizes for white supremacy, no other white identity is acceptable. An unfortunate by product has been the loss of cultural coherence. As Steele puts it: "After America admitted what was worst about itself, there was not enough [white moral] authority to support what was best." Consequently, when the false principles of racial superiority were cast aside, so also were the valid ones of personal responsibility, hard work, delayed gratification, commitment to excellence, competition by merit, and even truth.

Identity Politics dismisses the sacrifices that millions of Americans of all races have made to defend the principle of "equality under the law." It also ignores the two centuries of struggle that transformed this nation into the most inclusive, multi-ethnic, and multi-racial society in history. The popular notion that blacks are "marginalized" is preposterous. To the contrary, they are presently at the center of America's culture and consciousness.

During O. J. Simpson's 1994 murder trial, black defense attorney Jonnie Cochran brilliantly made it a contest between solid empirical evidence and white guilt. According to Steele, Cochran "gambled on the court's being obsessed with showing its utter freedom from racial bias ... Johnnie Cochran instinctively understood that the court—an American institution in the age of white guilt—was infinitely more concerned with its own moral authority and legitimacy than with the truth." It could only be seen as possessing moral authority if it shed all taint of racism, whether real or imagined.[11]

---

11 Shelby Steele, *White Guilt*, 41, 106-10; David Horowitz, *The Enemy* Within,

Such consequences continue presently. Whites, for example, cannot criticize black misbehavior without being accused of racism. Even though studies convincingly demonstrate that children from single parent, matriarchal families have more, and bigger, problems than do children from two parent homes, critics of such aberrant standards are condemned as sexist or racist. Consequently, black poverty has become the currency of legitimacy that encourages blacks to believe their personal stories are the only genuine interpretations of white-on-black racism. Everybody must sit down and shut up while they tell their stories. Any white who suggests that a two-way conversation, rather than a one-way lecture, might lead to a better understanding is shouted down as a racist.

To avoid such condemnation, most whites yield to silly racial policies without even realizing they are mostly trying to disassociate from racism. When a white girl's challenge to the affirmative action programs at the University of Michigan reached the Supreme Court in 2003, over one hundred institutions such as corporations, the military, state and local governments, and other universities submitted briefs in favor of racial preferences. Few based their arguments on a studied analysis of why minorities were unable to win places in the colleges of the brief-submitters without racial preferences.

In truth, the institutions were not interested in discovering the authentic explanations for minority non-competitiveness. They were interested only in winning legal validation for affirmative action as a way of demonstrating their disassociation with racism. Without racial preferences it would be too difficult to admit enough minorities to demonstrate their commitment to diversity. Moreover, according to Steele, "to conspicuously disassociate it must be clear that racial preferences were used. Most Ivy League universities want their freshmen classes to be roughly 8% black. This works as disassociation because they would be no more than 1% or 2% black without racial preferences... And once disassociated the institution goes about its business without worrying why minorities do so poorly in it."[12]

(Washington, D. C.: Regnery Publishing, 2021), 3, 6,7

12 Shelby Steele, *White Guilt*, 121-22, 129-30

The imperative for white leaders to disassociate from racism has already wrecked our public schools and is well on its way toward destroying colleges. For white college administrators and faculty, the sole purpose of affirmative action is to protect themselves collectively from charges of racism. Just as white guilt led institutions into attempts at substituting equality of outcomes for equality of opportunity it has also made social morality more important than individual morality.

During his presidency, Bill Clinton proudly wore a badge of social morality as the metaphorical first black President. He used it as a license to disregard individual morality, as evidenced by the Lewinsky affair. Thus, even as the political Left won moral authority for being socially concerned, it is unable to solve America's racial problems because it has alienated itself from the traditional values and principles required for success. In the sixty years since the 1960s Civil Rights Movement not a single President has articulated how blacks might so much as even share responsibility for their own advancement. Instead, they persistently focus on fabricating new racial preferences, much like an incompetent medic repetitively pulling new band aids out of a box to stop blood flow from a severed artery.[13]

Notwithstanding denials and contrary misrepresentations, Critical Race Theory, and/or its antiracist remedies, are indeed taught in law schools, colleges, and even elementary schools. They are also taught in the military, government institutions, and large corporations.

Since the turn of the 20th-into-the-21st century, academic literature about the methods of K-12 education have focused on storytelling, a hallmark of Critical Race Theory. Narrative stories from personal experiences are particularly used to familiarize white children with the challenges of blacks and other minorities and even allegedly victimized majorities such as girls. But the storytelling is a one-way street. White boys may participate only by sitting still and listening, or by writing papers to detail their privileges. One storytelling advocate writes, "The use of voice, or 'naming your reality' is a way that CRT links form and substance in scholarship... Much of reality is socially constructed. Critical Race Theory sees the official school curriculum as a culturally specific artifact designed to maintain a White supremacist master script."

---

13   Shelby Steele, *White Guilt*, 56, 152, 162-63, 176

In truth, however, David Horowitz explains: "... 'white privilege' is a fiction convenient to the Left whose real agenda is to demonize white people and remove all others from responsibility for what they do or fail to accomplish in life. 'White privilege' is not an analytic category; it is a weapon designed to cripple and destroy white people who get in the way of the Leftist agenda."

Public schools are progressively integrating CRT material into instruction. After vetoing a bill to include an ethnic studies requirement in all California high schools in 2018, Governor Gavin Newsom signed a bill in October 2021 to make the course a requirement for the 2029-30 graduating class. Elective courses will be available for the 2025-26 graduating class. The courses are expected to address race from the perspective of how a white dominated culture affects racism. They are also expected to have an entire section devoted to "intersectionality," which enables a victim to gain additional points in the Victimhood Olympics merely by being a member of more than one alleged victim group. One example might be a black woman, who is supposedly doubly oppressed because she is both black and female. During its proposal stage, a former U.S. Department of Education official editorialized in the *Wall Street Journal*, "The proponents of [California's] ethnic studies are so insulated by Marxism and Identity Politics, that they miss insights from other fields."

In 2017 the Seattle Public School Board created an "Ethnic Studies Task Force" in order to make the schools more inclusive for students "of color." The task force drafted objectives that overflow with CRT buzzwords and phrases such as "critiques of systems of oppression... to include colonialism, racism, patriarchy and capitalism" and a goal "to dismantle White supremacy and institutional racism." Ohio's State Education Board adopted a resolution to "offer training to Board members to identify our own implicit biases ... and to require training for all state employees and contractors working for the Department of Education to identify their own implicit biases."

The above initiatives are misdirected. They come at a time when 82% of black fourth graders read below a basic level as compared to 54% of white fourth graders. A 2010 Pew Research report disclosed that more blacks aged 20-34 without high school diplomas are in prison than employed. Teachers are failing black youths when they instruct them to name "their own reality."[14]

In the summer of 2021 America's largest teacher's union announced a plan to promote CRT in all fifty states and 14,000 local school districts. Representing three million teachers at its annual conference, the National Education Association (NEA) approved funding for three CRT-related items. First, is implementing CRT in the K-12 curricula. Second, is promoting it in the local school districts. Third, and most cynical, is a fund to attack opponents of CRT, including politically conservative research groups.

Until the announcement, mainstream TV commentators and newspaper editorialists were denying that Critical Race Theory was taught in K-12 schools. Many still do. It has been a persistent bad faith claim that the NEA's announcement finally contradicted. The Association also agreed to oppose legislative restrictions on teaching CRT. The delegates pledged to "join with Black Lives Matter ... and the Zinn Education Project" on George Floyd's birthday for political demonstrations and to "teach lessons about structural racism and oppression." Finally, the NEA resolved to "research the organizations" opposing CRT and supply operatives for attacking them.

Although the NEA proclaims their CRT advocacy is a matter of high-minded principle regarding the truth about America, a couple of demographic facts may reveal the true unspoken reasons teachers want to promote it. First, nearly 80% public school teachers are women. Since CRT endorses feminism, teacher support for CRT may be an indirect way of supporting more "equitable treatment" (meaning higher pay) for themselves. In *How to Be an Antiracist,* Ibram Kendi writes, "To truly be feminist is to be antiracist." Second, about 18% of the teachers are non-white.

In response to a letter from the National School Boards Association in October 2021, Attorney General Merrick Garland directed the FBI to assist local law enforcement to investigate "harassment" and

---

14   David Horowitz, *The Enemy Within,* 16-17; Jonathan Butcher and Mike Gonzalez, "Critical Race Theory, the New Intolerance, and It's Grip on America," *Heritage Foundation,* (December 7, 2020), 15-18: https://tinyurl.com/2p9fcm9k; Jocelyn Gecker, "Ethnic Studies Made High School Requirement," *Associated Press,* (October 8, 2021): https://tinyurl.com/53ypsaze

"intimidation" of local school board officials. It is unclear whether parents who merely speak out against Critical Race Theory and the COVID-19 masking of school children constitute "harassment" or "intimidation" in the context of Garland's instructions. Nonetheless, his memo ordered the FBI and U.S. attorneys to arrange meetings with federal, state, and local leaders within the month.

The initiative was a chilling attack on free speech. Many parents may be deterred from attending such meetings when they know the FBI will be watching. Even those brave enough to attend may be intimidated to speak their minds. Yet censorship is precisely what K-12 teachers, as well as college professors, promote as Leftist gospel. According to the Foundation for Individual Rights (FIRE), ninety percent of public colleges maintain policies that don't live up to their free speech obligations under the First Amendment.

CRT opponent Chris Rufo editorialized in the *New York Post* that the NSBA's letter was full of lies and exaggerations. "It begins with the claim that 'critical race theory is not taught in public schools,' despite a vast body of evidence showing that CRT is widespread in public schools. Even the NEA admitted it." Rufo continues, "The NSBA deliberately misrepresents debates at school board meetings as 'threats' and angry speech as 'violence.' Their letter refers to dozens of news stories alluding to 'disruptions', 'shouts,' 'arguments,' and 'mobs but, contrary to its core claim, cites only a single example of actual violence against a school official... The purpose of mobilizing the FBI is not only to monitor dissent but to subdue it. The [NSBA's] suggestion that parents might be engaging in 'domestic terrorism' is designed to suppress speech and assembly and to justify the further federalization of education policy."

Late in year 2020, Seattle Public Schools held a teachers' training session in which American schools were deemed guilty of "spirit murder" against black students. It also taught that America is a "race-based white-supremist society built by kidnapped black slaves, which created the profits that created our nation." White teachers were taught that they must apologize for their guilt of whiteness and become antiracist educators.

Also late in 2020, the San Diego Public Schools got radicalized. The applicable union's objective was to turn the city's schools into an antiracist school district. In one training session white teachers were

15

told "you are racist." Trainers told them they must confess their white privilege and convince others to see it. In a second presentation white teachers were told: "Whiteness reproduces poverty, failing schools, high unemployment, school closings, and trauma for people of color."

About the same time third graders in Apple's California hometown of Cupertino were taught to "deconstruct" their racial identities, then rank themselves based on power and privilege. They were taught that white men were at the top of the "intersectional" privilege totem pole whereas black women were near the bottom. White boys were then told that when they became adults, they would automatically possess unearned privilege even though the school ranks among the state's top one percent academically because it's majority is Asian American, not majority white.

One Chinese American Cupertino parent remarked that the exercise was reminiscent of the Chinese Cultural Revolution under dictator Mao Zedong. "[It divides society between] the oppressor and the oppressed, and since these identities are inborn characteristics, people cannot change. The only way to change it is via violent revolution. Growing up in China, I had learned it many times. The outcome is the family will be ripped apart; husband hates wife, children hate parents. I think it is already happening here." Consider the irony of teaching blacks to hate America, the very system that freed the slaves and made our country's blacks the freest, richest, and most privileged black citizens in the World.

Lest the reader infer that such radicalism is isolated on the Left coast, a training secession deep in the Ozarks at Springfield, Missouri was conspicuously hostile. Trainers taught that funding education from property tax is inherently racist as was any "colorblindness" claim of being indifferent to a person's color. Minority themed Halloween costumes were deemed to be racist like KKK costumes, only more socially acceptable.

CRT proselytizers are also fond of quoting so-called hate crime statistics. By 2020 forty-seven of the fifty states had such dubious crimes on their books. Reformed American Communist Party member David Horowitz writes, "A hate crime is a thought crime. Every totalitarian regime in history from the Spanish Inquisition to the Stalinist Show Trials has outlawed unwanted thought. In Stalin's Russia, being 'anti-Soviet' was a thought crime for which tens of millions were dispatched to the concentration camps and firing squads... If [American] citizens cannot form and express opinions freely, they will lose the ability to defend their other freedoms. To go from prosecuting 'hate crimes' to banning 'hate speech' is a small step—and an inevitable one toward the establishment of a totalitarian order."

Similarly, a Philadelphia elementary school that is 94% black forced fifth graders to celebrate "black communism" and simulate a Black Power rally in honor of Angela Davis, a once-notorious political activist. Although only 13% of the school's students achieve basic literacy at graduation, its teachers have abandoned traditional teaching in favor of radical political activism.

In February 2020, North Carolina's Wake County School system had a similar training system. Two hundred teachers of a school district serving the state capital of Raleigh with a one million dollar annual budget for its Office of Equity Affairs attended the training. Teachers were instructed to ignore parental concerns about the ideology of antiracism. "You can't let parents deter you" because the children of white parents benefit from the racist system of whiteness and are "not learning at home about diversity." In short, teachers are urged to sabotage parental wishes.[15]

Perhaps beginning with O. J. Simpson's murder trial in 1994 America's growing obsession with Identity Politics has distracted our leaders from more important concerns. The shameful debacle that was the Afghanistan withdrawal in 2021 was but one example. Barely two months before the farce, Joint Chiefs of Staff Chairman General Mark Milley revealed that he had apparently become more involved studying Identity Politics than in planning the Afghanistan evacuation. When asked whether he agreed with West Point's practice of teaching Critical Race Theory to the cadets, the general affirmed his agreement, because it was important for the Army to understand "white rage." He considered the January 6, 2021, capitol occupation as a manifestation of such rage.

---

15 Ibram Kendi, *How to Be an Antiracist*, 189; David Horowitz, *The Enemy Within*, 53, 80, 154; Christopher Rufo, "Liberals were losing the argument over critical race theory in schools—Time to Call in the FBI," *New York Post*, (October 6, 2021); "Christopher Rufo on Woke Education," *City Journal*, : https://tinyurl.com/ms4a7vx3

Instead, the January 6, 2021 incident reflected two factors. First, was anger that law enforcement, big city municipalities, the media, and the Democrat Party generally fabricated excuses for the black rioters, looters, and arsonists and their allies that ran amok during the summer of 2020. Even though anti-COVID social distancing was the norm, politicians exempted rioters, but not church members wanting to attend Sunday services. Second, millions of voters were aware that the mainstream media and big consumer-facing technology companies were biased against President Donald Trump's reelection and restricted the flow of information detrimental to Joe Biden's candidacy. Perhaps the most notable example was the incident involving his son Hunter's laptop computer that had been turned over to the FBI. Only days before the election, National Public Radio refused to carry the story and Twitter removed it from the *New York Post's* Twitter stream.

Provocative incidents like those cited above require an explanation about how they materialized, which entails a basic understanding of Critical Race Theory and how it evolved.

CHAPTER TWO:

CRITICAL RACE THEORY

RECALL THAT CRITICAL RACE THEORY is a race-specific derivative of Critical Theory. The latter originated with the Neo-Marxist Frankfurt School of sociology in 1923 Germany. Its purpose was to learn why communism was not spreading from 1917 Russia to more industrialized countries as Marxist theory predicted. The Frankfurt Neo-Marxists concluded the problem was Western Culture. To provoke a communist revolution in a Western industrialized country, revolutionaries must first undermine the culture from within. Even though Marxist theory specifies that societies will always be composed of victim and oppressor classes, Western prosperity prevented too many workers from discerning their victim status relative to capitalists. The Frankfurt group, therefore, had to find other cleavage lines to dismantle the culture. Even though Adolph Hitler demonstrated the power of race as a fracture contour, the Frankfurt scholars overlooked it even as they fled to New York's Columbia University to escape Nazism. Their American successors would discover race and gender as useful fault lines in the 1960s and 70s.[1]

CRT originated as Critical Legal Studies (CLS) in the 1970s when pioneering law professors published papers claiming that America's legal system operated for the benefit of white men because it was written by white men. Among the CLS authors was Harvard's Derrick Bell who published *Race, Racism and American Law* in 1973. Bell and his colleagues argued that America's legal apparatus was systemically biased. Consequently, they interpreted equality under the law as camouflage for white supremacy, patriarchy, and racial oppression.

---

1 Mark Levin, *American Marxism,* (New York, Threshold Editions, 2021), 82; Jonathan Butcher and Mike Gonzalez, "Critical Race Theory, the New Intolerance, and It's Grip on America," *Heritage Foundation,* (December 7, 2020), 3-5.

In 1989 Harvard's Kimberlé Crenshaw introduced a hierarchal concept of victimhood ostentatiously termed "intersectionality." A black woman, she argues, is doubly oppressed because she stands at the intersection of two victim groups: black and female. Her 1989 paper objected to a 1976 ruling by a white female judge against five black women plaintiffs in a discrimination case against General Motors. The judge ruled that the plaintiffs needed to win their case based on their race or gender, not a combination of both. In part the ruling read: "The legislative history surrounding Title VII [of the 1964 Civil Rights Act] does not indicate that the goal of the statute was to create a new classification of 'black women' who would have greater standing than, for example, a black male. The prospect of the creation of new classes of protected minorities, governed only by the mathematical principles of permutation and combination, [i.e., intersectionality] clearly raises the prospect of opening the hackneyed Pandora's box."[2]

Nevertheless, Crenshaw's intersectionality concept became the wellspring for Identity Politics. In time entire academic disciplines involving Gender Studies, Black Studies, Ethnic Studies, Gay Studies, Critical Race Studies, and Post-Colonial Studies grew from Bell's cynical views. A 1993 *Harvard Law Review* article by Bell acolyte Cheryl Harris equated whiteness with property ownership. Consequently, she recommended suspending private property rights so that land and wealth might be seized from the rich and redistributed along racial lines.

The Democrat Party sprang upon Identity Politics to form a coalition of victim groups comprising blacks, ethnic minorities, and feminists. They fashioned Identity Politics into a totem pole of privilege in which the value of one's opinion is *inversely* proportional to their location on the pole. Heterosexual white males are at the top whereas black lesbians—or some other multiple intersectional victim group—is at the bottom. Professor Jonathan Haidt explained, "America is a giant matrix of oppression where its victims cannot fight their battles separately. They must all come together to fight their common enemy, the group that sits at the top of the oppression pyramid: the straight white male. That is why a perceived slight against one victim

---

2 Jane Coaston, "The Intersectionality Wars," *Vox*, May 28, 2019: https://tinyurl.com/bdhrtncm;

group calls forth protest from all victim groups." In 2018 the National Science Foundation supported over 100 programs to combat so-called intersectional oppression in the sciences alone at a cost of $63 million.

Sometimes, however, the victim groups come into conflict with one another. When that happens, the winner must be determined by reference to the oppression matrix. ESPN's job assignment decision in 2021 to favor black basketball commentator Maria Taylor over white Rachel Nichols reveals the extra victimhood points black women get compared to white women.[3]

In their 2001 formative *Critical Race Theory,* pioneering scholars Richard Delgado and Jean Stefancic defined CRT as follows:

> The Critical Race Theory movement is a collection of activists and scholars engaged in studying and transforming the relationship among race, racism, and power. The movement considers many of the same issues that conventional civil rights and ethnic studies discourses take up but places them in a broader perspective that includes economics, history, setting, group, self-interest, emotions, and the unconscious. Unlike traditional civil rights discourse, which stresses incrementalism and step-by-step progress, CRT questions the very foundations of the liberal order, including, equality theory, legal reasoning, Enlightenment rationalism, and neutral principles of constitutional law.[4]

Several points about their definition warrant comment.

First, they describe Critical Race Theory as a movement, not an academic discipline. Thus, students are not merely studying to learn, but to fundamentally change American law and society. They enter the field with a predetermined agenda, thereby corrupting objectivity. Second, the discipline covers several perspectives including some that are prone to speculative inferences and demagoguery such "emotions and the unconscious." Such vague factors can easily be misinterpreted

---

3 David Horowitz, *The Enemy Within,* 22-23; Kevin Draper, "A Disparaging Video Prompts a Fallout at ESPN," *New York Times,* (July 4, 2021): https://tinyurl.com/222sscup

4 Richard Delgado and Jean Sefancic, *Critical Race Theory: Third Edition,* (New York, NYU Press, 2017), 3

to fit a preset agenda. Third, CRT shuns a gradual process toward its goals. Instead, it seeks to overturn some of America's treasured foundations including equality of opportunity and replace it with a pseudo collective equality for groups. In short, it seeks to dismantle America's traditional culture from within, just as the Frankfurt School wanted to do in Europe in the 1920s and 30s.

Critical Race Theory emerged during the 1970s when several black scholars grew frustrated that the civil rights advances of the 1960s had apparently stalled. As most affirmative action students failed to perform well academically, for example, the professors rejected arguments that the black student performance was as much each student's individual responsibility as a societal one. Consequently, they initiated a witch hunt to find other explanations thereby enabling affirmative action participants to evade personal responsibility.

As a result, Derrick Bell claimed he discovered a diabolical method of white suppression that predecessors had missed. He elaborately termed it "interest convergence." As an example, he argued that the 1954 *Brown v. Topeka Board of Education* Supreme Court ruling ending racial segregation resulted more from the self-interest of elite whites than from their desire to help blacks. Since both blacks and white elites interpreted racial integration as beneficial to their respective interests, their interests "converged." When he examined the Brown case background, Bell learned that the NAACP had been litigating school desegregation suits for years with little result. Why, he asked, had the Supreme Court unexpectedly given blacks everything they had been asking for in the Brown case? He concluded that white considerations over global and domestic politics, not altruism, prompted the Court's ruling.

In 1954 the Korean and Second World Wars were recent memories. Many soldiers returned after having for the first time experienced a setting in which cooperation for survival superseded racial considerations. America's leaders concluded that black men could not be expected to willingly go home to a perpetual Jim Crow environment. Any attempt to force them might result in violence.

Simultaneously the United States was locked in a Cold War with international communism. America and the Soviet Union fought for global influence diplomatically instead of with guns and rockets. Each sought to win the loyalties of emerging Third World nations, many of which were predominately composed of black, brown, or Asian people. America could ill-afford for the global press to carry stories of lynchings, KKK violence, and racist law enforcement. Years later Delgado and Stefancic cited an independent study suggesting that Bell's cynical interpretation was correct: "When the Justice Department intervened on the side of the NAACP ... it was responding to a flood of secret cables outlining America's interest in improving its image in the eyes of the Third World."[5]

Historian Paul Johnson has a contrary interpretation. America's Founding Fathers based our judicial system on English Common Law and a statutory tradition. Common Law is derived from custom and judicial precedent whereas statute law is passed by a legislature or some other governing bodies. Judges interpreted common law and administered statute law. Although English judges had interpreted law through the lens of equity, meaning fairness, they had done so by understanding that equity should be no more than "the correction ... wherein the law is deficient." But equity was not omnipotent.

Among the English legal scholars who most influenced the Founding Fathers was William Blackstone who wrote: "The liberty of considering all cases in an equitable light must not be indulged too far lest ... we destroy all law and leave every decision entirely to the breast of the judge. And law without equity, though hard and disagreeable, is much more desirable... than equity without law, which would make every judge a legislator and introduce infinite confusion."[6]

For over a hundred and fifty years the Supreme Court had been careful to heed Blackstone's warning. By the late 1940s, however, many Americans regretted that blacks had failed to participate fully in the country's political life and were often required to attend racially segregated public schools. As a result, the 1954 *Brown* case was perhaps the Court's most important ruling. When concluding that racially segregated public schools violated the equal protection guarantees of the Fourteenth Amendment, one justice wrote: "I suppose that the reason this case is here is that action couldn't be

---

5 Delgado and Stefancic, 22-24

6 Paul Johnson, *A History of the American People,* (New York, Harper Perennial, 1997), 951-52

obtained through Congress." Thus, he reasoned, the justices could intervene to correct what they saw as a failure of the legislature and authorized the federal courts to supervise the desegregation process.

Therefore, in *Brown* the Court not only made the law, but also enforced it. That was no small matter. As late as 1994, four-hundred-and-fifty school districts were still under federal supervision. Entire generations of children grew up in schools managed by a federal court instead of a locally elected school board.[7]

More recently the federal Justice Department (DOJ) has similarly intervened to exercise control over selected municipal police departments suspected of racial discrimination. In the year 2000, it started an investigation in Los Angeles that cost taxpayers over $100 million and lasted twelve years. Under terms of a consent decree, Los Angeles police could hardly speak to a civilian without filing numerous forms documenting each incident. The LAPD spent $50 million annually over several years and pulled 350 officers from the streets to meet the decree's mountainous paperwork.

The prime beneficiaries have been temporary workers, termed "police monitors." They report compliance to the federal courts and collect enormous fees. One Detroit monitor amassed $13 million before the city even tried to recover the funds after learning she had been consorting with the mayor. The New Jersey State Police spent $36 million on a monitoring system and $70 million running it. Partly to accommodate similar oversight, Oakland police had to allocate 18 officers to "internal affairs" as compared to only 11 in its homicide division.

Federal attorneys have sometimes been frivolous in choosing which municipalities to investigate. According to Heather MacDonald's *War on Cops,* one DOJ attorney remarked, "I feel like going to Seattle and my Google sweep picked a few articles on the police there." Another said, "My buddy at the NAACP ... called me and asked us to open an investigation in Des Moines." Once the attorneys show-up they can launch a multi-year fishing expedition involving thousands of documents without ever explaining what they are looking for.[8]

---

7 Paul Johnson, *A History of the American People*, 953

8 Heather MacDonald, *The War on Cops,* (New York, Encounter Books, 2016), 85-86, 90-91

Ten years after the *Brown* decision, Congress passed the 1964 Civil Rights Act, which specifically forbade racial quotas. The Act also created the Equal Employment Opportunity Commission as an enforcement agency. Despite its original marching orders, by 1971 the commission was imposing quotas as remedies for "protected minorities." Without being a "protected minority" (e.g., black, Hispanic, Asian, or female) white males had no legal standing to sue when they were discriminated against.

Contrary to Derrick Bell's thesis, the 1954 ruling was a boon for racial minorities and a bane for America's traditional elite because it enabled judges to legislate from the bench. Moreover, it was eventually followed by an enormous race-quota compliance bureaucracy. Among the Deep State entities focused on civil rights are: Civil Rights Commission, Equal Opportunity Employment Commission, Labor Department's Office of Federal Contract Compliance Programs, and Office of Minority Business Enterprise. Additionally, there are large civil rights offices in federal departments such as Justice, Defense, and Health, Education and Welfare. Notwithstanding a diversity mission, the Deep State civil rights bureaucracies ignored racial quotas for themselves and are overwhelmingly staffed with blacks and other minorities.[9]

The interest convergence thesis that led Bell to his white supremacy theory about the *Brown* ruling stems from two bogus CRT tenets. The first is that racism is ordinary, not aberrational. It is the common, everyday experience of blacks. The second is that white-over-black ascendency serves multiple purposes for whites.

According to Delgado the first tenet means that whites normally don't recognize racism. He even claims that whites who are "colorblind" to skin pigmentation don't understand the everyday racism that blacks experience. Instead, claims Delgado, blacks must explain it to whites. He writes, "[Racial minorities] may be able to communicate to their white counterparts matters that the whites are unlikely to know. Minority status, in other words, brings with it a presumed competence to speak about race and racism," which whites cannot have. Since the minorities are presumed to be powerless victims, they cannot themselves be racist. Consequently, when CRT advocates tell whites that the two sides must have a conversation about race, they are really

---

9 Paul Johnson, *A History of the American People*, 953, 955

saying, "Shut up while I lecture you concerning all of my complaints about your racism." Learning about racism is a one-way street from black to white. After fifty-five years of The War on Poverty, however, this CRT tenet seems feeble. In truth, it promotes a false belief in perpetual black victimhood.

Even though alleged antiblack racism is not now as obvious as during segregation, CRT claims that "storytelling" from the lived experiences of today's blacks reveals that racism continues to blight their lives. Encounters with police remain problematic. While the prison population is mostly black, CEOs, surgeons, senators, and university presidents are almost all white. Oscar winning actors are mostly white. Blacks have shorter lifespans, receive worse medical care, have fewer academic credentials, and comprise a disproportionate share of the poor. O. J. Simpson avoided a double-murder conviction due to similar "storytelling."[10]

CRT contends that the consequences noted above result from systemic racism as opposed to the collective behavior of blacks. Nevertheless, many blacks are raised in a dysfunctional culture. Seventy percent of black children in 2018 were born out of wedlock as compared to 52% of Hispanics, 28% of whites, and 12% of Asians. By comparison, in 1965 only 24% of black infants and 3% of white infants were born to single mothers. In 2013 California's black elementary school students were truant four times more often than whites. Black males between the ages of 14 to 17 are killed by shootings at six times the rate of white and Hispanic teenage males combined. Within America's seventy-five most populous counties in 2009, blacks accounted for 15% of the population, but 62% of robberies, 57% of murders and 45% of assaults. Delgado admits that "sixty percent of the black men in the District of Columbia are enmeshed in [the criminal justice] system—in jail, or prison, on probation or parole, or wanted on a warrant ... [and] the number of black men in prison or jail is larger than the number attending college."[11]

---

10 Delgado and Stefancic, *Critical Race Theory*, 8-11

11 Roger Clegg, "Percentage of Births to Unmarried Women," *Center for Equal Opportunity*. (February 26, 2020): https://tinyurl.com/mvmwnhrd; Heather MacDonald, *Diversity*, 78; Delgado and Stefancic, *Critical Race* Theory, 120; George Akerlof and Janet Yellen, "An Analysis of Out of Wedlock Births in the United States," *Brookings Institute,* (August 1, 1996): https://tinyurl.com/49c77dsx; Heather MacDonald, *War,* 30, 49, 73; Jason Amos,

Heather MacDonald suggests that policy makers ponder a thought experiment before concluding that systemic racism is responsible for the academic and economic underperformance of blacks. "If American blacks acted *en masse* like Asian Americans for ten years in all things relevant to economic success—if they had similar rates of school attendance, paying attention in class, doing homework and studying for exams, staying away from crime, persisting in a job, and avoiding out-of-wedlock childbearing—and we *still* saw racial differences in income, professional status, and incarceration rates, [only] then would it be well justified to seek an explanation in unconscious prejudice."[12]

In response, Delgado's devotees point to dubious "newer" forms of racism such as microaggressions and hate speech, which they demand be answered with safe spaces and speech censorship. Other minority races and ethnic groups must also be protected from microaggressions and hate speech. The same applies to "protected gender classes," which include all so-called genders except heterosexual white males. Delgado defines microaggressions as "Stunningly small encounters with racism usually unnoticed by members of the majority race." According to a UCLA list, the following are microaggressions:[13]

There is only one race, the human race. The comment supposedly denies the significance of a minority person's race.

America is a melting pot. The remark assumes non-white immigrants will assimilate into our society as opposed to segregating in their own enclaves where they speak their own language and minimize contacts with other races. The "nationalist" branch of CRT believes their loyalty should be first to their community and only secondarily to America.[14]

America is the land of opportunity. The sentence implies that minority races are not taking advantage of America's opportunities because they are lazy or incompetent.

"Young Black Men Without High School Diplomas," *Pew Research,* (October 10, 2010): https://tinyurl.com/3ffykxbm

12 Heather MacDonald, *Diversity,* 107

13 UCLA Microaggression List (2014): https://tinyurl.com/2p94mkyv;

14 Delgado and Stefancic, *Critical Race Theory,* 69

According to Delgado, hate speech encompasses: "Racial slurs and epithets or other harsh language that has no purpose other than to demean and marginalize other people or groups." An expression that includes the N-word is a classic example. Insulting terms such as Hillbilly, Redneck, Hayseed, Good-'ole-Boy, and Bubba do not qualify because they discriminate against white males. Much as with microaggressions, only protected classes, such as blacks and feminists, are permitted to define hate speech terms. The passive remedy for hate speech is safe spaces. The active remedy is censorship and cancel culture. According to Mark Potok of the Southern Poverty Law Center, "Our aim in life is to destroy these [typically white male conservative] groups. To completely destroy them."[15]

While widespread academic endorsement of Critical Race Theory, microaggressions, censorship, and safe spaces presently dismays many Americans, Shelby Steele explains how they gained traction, but not legitimacy. Recall that Steele had a black father and white mother. Additionally, his education mostly predates affirmative action, which he opposes. His 2006 *White Guilt* explains how the guilt elite whites felt when America moved out of its long age of white supremacy in the mid 1960s enabled race hustlers to blackmail the rest of America for racial preferences.

Although correct to admit their prior race relations failures, whites lost moral authority when they acknowledged them in the 1960s. Since they could not lead without moral authority, whites had to create it in some new way to prove they were not racist. As a result, since the mid-1960s most every kind of American institution has proclaimed its devotion to racial diversity. To refute the racist stigma that would enable whites to retain their leadership positions, the institutions started using racial preferences to increase the visibility of minorities.

White fear of stigmatization enabled radical African American activists to redefine racism in increasingly trivial and imagined ways such as microaggressions and systemic racism. They saw an opportunity to blackmail white elites to give blacks special privileges. In the Critical Race Theory model of victimized blacks and oppressor whites, the stars aligned to provide a rare extortion opportunity. Under

---

15 Delgado and Stefancic, *Critical Race Theory*, 175; David Horowitz, *The Enemy Within*, 87

such circumstances, the oppressed only act out their anger when they perceive weakness in the oppressor. Blacks did not often act out their anger during slavery and segregation, because the oppressor's power was too large. "Anger in the oppressed," wrote Steele, "is a response to perceived opportunity, not injustice. And expressions of anger escalate not with more injustice, but with *less* injustice."[16]

By the mid 1960s white guilt created a new kind of black leadership unlike that of the selfless Martin Luther King that appealed to America's best instincts. The new leaders were smaller men specializing in moral indignation who could profit from white guilt. "Lacking other sources of capital," says Steele, "blacks embraced racism as power itself... [Consequently,] Global racism seeks to make every racist event the tip of an iceberg so that the redress will be to the measure of the iceberg rather than the measure of its tip." By the end of the twentieth century black students who had never suffered discrimination, much less been beaten by a white policeman, enjoyed the systemic redress of affirmative action with a new sense of entitlement. Even Delgado notes that CRT's influence has been most beneficial for black elites, like college students, instead of ordinary blacks. He confesses CRT is too much focused on microaggressions, racial insults, unconscious discrimination, and affirmative action in higher education.[17]

Although the 2020 riots destroyed black neighborhoods, they transformed mostly dubious accusations of police brutality against blacks into a global debate that amplified white guilt and expanded black power. They transformed antiblack discriminatory events between the participants into the "impersonal" and "structural" forces of systemic racism. Even though whites compose less than half of the police officers in cities like New York, the rioters knew that they could frame the racism to the scale of white guilt instead of framing it to the actual scale of white racism, which was too small to count for much.

While today's black college students complain to Steele that racism is systemically all around them when he asks for examples, they can rarely provide any other than things that require a new definition of racism for a man with Steele's history. The so-called global racism they perceive today allows black students to live on a campus notorious

---

16 Shelby Steele, *White Guilt*, (New York: Harper Perennial, 2006), 20, 21, 27

17 Delgado and Stfancic, *Critical Race Theory*, 107

for censoring voices like Steele's while simultaneously feeling more aggrieved than the black students of sixty years ago, which was before the true civil rights victories. Thus, even when a college announces new commitments to diversity, it merely increases the resentment of its entitled minority students. White guilt empowers the so-called oppressed black students to silence any white critic by merely playing the race card.[18]

Delgado's second CRT tenet concerning white-over-black ascendency yields Derrick Bell's "interest convergence" theory. Thus, Bell criticizes whites for accommodating black militants only out of self-interest. Yet CRT proponents seldom note that blacks are also only acting in their own self-interest. Since "interest convergence" implies that both races are pursuing self-interest, one is no more ethical than the other.

But when blacks continually play the race card to blackmail whites into providing evermore preferences to racial minorities, black motives are indeed unethical. Any group that relies upon a platform of microaggressions, safe spaces, and cancel culture must ultimately lose its moral authority in a democracy. Governing race relations without regard to the opinions of the majority may therefore be the reason some CRT proponents want to form a totalitarian entity to decree those relations, as with Ibram Kendi's proposed Department of Antiracism (DOA).

The Department would need to be authorized by a new constitutional amendment. It would be staffed by so-called experts trained in antiracism, which is mostly a new definition of racism designed to yield minorities the power to increasingly gain racial preferences until the economic, educational, and health status of all races are equal collectively. It would be sanctioned to nullify, veto, or abolish any law involving race. It would be unaccountable to voters or any branch of the federal government. In short, on racial matters it would be dictatorial and therefore more powerful than any other federal branch.[19]

---

18 Shelby Steele, *White Guilt*, 35-40; David Horowitz, *The Enemy Within*, 41, 45

19 Ibram Kendi, "Pass an Anti-Racist Constitutional Amendment," *Politico*: https://tinyurl.com/3dmk5ajw;

In principle there's nothing wrong with teaching Critical Race Theory as a possible explanation for America's racial history, but it should not be represented as the only valid explanation. In fact, CRT has serious flaws.

First, it invites followers to naval gaze in a manner that leads to delusion. CRT's instruction that blacks explain their experience with racism through one-way "storytelling" leaves them with no appreciation for the white perspective. Consequently, they are dismissive of white contributions to American history, which they regard as having been accomplished in a cakewalk. CRT encourages such thinking because it keeps blacks focused on victimhood, the source of their power. In truth, white pioneers endured considerable hardship to open new regions of our country and over 600,000 overwhelmingly white American soldiers were killed in the Civil War, which ended up freeing the slaves.

Popular black authors like Ta-Nehisi Coates and Ibram Kendi show little understanding of the white experience. In his autobiographical *How to Be an Antiracist,* Kendi writes of his dislike for three isolated white students in his predominantly black elementary school because they grouped in the front row of his class. His presumed they aspired to be the teachers' pets, although they may merely have been eager to learn. In contrast, white Southern authors such as John Grisham, Harper Lee, Joe David Brown, William Faulkner, Gene Dattel, Pat Conroy, Larry McMurtry, and Carson McCullers promote an understanding of black victimhood. They changed the course of history by teaching other whites to re-examine their comprehension of black perspectives. Unfortunately, few black authors try to help other blacks understand the white viewpoint. CRT's self-centeredness only intensifies that problem.[20]

Second, CRT not only rewrites history it attempts to rewrite reality. It is one thing to focus on the black experience in American history, but it is quite another to represent opinion as fact and even make things up. Washington and Lee law professor and CRT instructor, Brandon Hasbrouck, wrote in a law review article that Robert E. Lee "was a monster. Black bodies were desecrated, and skin mutilated by Lee himself." Yet, Hasbrouck's cited source makes no mention of body

---

20 Ibram Kendi, *How to Be an Antiracist,* 45

desiccation or skin mutilation. Similarly, Nicole Hannah-Jones, who directed the *New York Times'* "1619 Project," has even erroneously claimed that the defense of slavery was "one primary reason the colonists fought the American Revolution."[21]

Third, rewriting an agenda-based version of history does not create a new reality. The remedies proposed for the injustices in the imagined new reality are extreme. Ultimately, they lead to totalitarianism in which control over race relations is progressively concentrated in Washington where so-called racial justice is managed by a Deep State of bureaucrats unaccountable to the voters. Censorship will silence dissenters. Similar models have been tried before, but don't work. Repeated attempts at communism, for example, provided disastrous outcomes including the deaths of a ten's-of-millions under totalitarian regimes in the twentieth century. Much as with Marxism, CRT's pursuit of a utopian future leads to a dystopian reality where only a ruling elite prospers.

Fourth, Critical Race Theory is racially divisive. It is designed to incite envy, resentment, and even hatred toward the so-called oppressor class, regardless of the individual opinions and behavior of class members. Defining our society as one split into factions of victims and oppressors cannot lead to unity, unless one side surrenders. That is too much to expect for a theory that releases an entire victim class from personal responsibility for their own performance. David Horowitz asks, "Remove the metaphysics of 'oppression' from this equation and what is left but a curriculum of hate that justifies aggression toward groups guilty by virtue of their skin color, class, gender or religion?"

CRT remedies such as persistent demands for equality of outcomes are creating consequences that are both bizarre and evil. Releasing black criminals from jail may equalize the number of blacks and whites in prison, for example, but it creates a more dangerous society. Consider how attempts to equalize the racial composition of the incarcerated enabled a 39-year-old black criminal with multiple offenses to avoid jail only weeks before he drove his car through a Christmas parade

---

21 Arijeta Lajka, "Robert E. Lee Owned Slaves," *Associated Press*, (June 12, 2020): https://tinyurl.com/ms47hr6;

Jonathan Butcher, "The *New York Times* Has Started Correcting the Historical Record in the '1619 Project," *Heritage Foundation*, (May 16, 2020): https://tinyurl.com/vzk8rbdz;

in Waukesha, Wisconsin, killing six people including one ten-year-old. Since black violent crime convictions are three-to-four times larger than their proportionate share of the population in America's largest 75 cities, unilateral changes in the collective behavior of blacks seems a better way to correct the disparate incarceration percentages. Undoubtedly, the media images of the lawlessness and looting during the riots following the George Floyd death suggests that irresponsibility and disregard for the most basic laws is a bigger cause of disparate racial incarceration than the tenets of Critical Race Theory.

Fifth, the Theory's presumption of systemic racism is mostly false. President Barack Obama's 2008 election and 2012 re-election are compelling evidence that most white Americans are not racist. During his presidency blacks represented but 13% of our nation's population compared to 62% for whites. Obama could not have been elected without considerable white support. In 2008 he won 43% of white votes and did almost as well with 41% in 2012. As a measure of progress, consider that not a solitary majority black, brown, or Asian nation in the World has elected a white President.

In the 2008 presidential election, white Americans fully lived up to the equality principle of the Declaration of Independence. It was not whites who manipulated blacks for power, it was Barack Obama. During the early primary season when he badly needed victories to be recognized as a serious candidate, he travelled to the Mississippi Delta where blacks are a significant majority. He told them, "I promise when I am President of the United States, I'll come back to the Delta." He never returned during his two-term presidency.

Instead of presuming systemic racism, it's more likely that America has evolved into a mostly post racial society. In fact, a Jamaican-born Harvard Professor, Orlando Patterson, concludes "[America] is the least racist white-majority society in the World; has a better record of legal protections than any other society, white or black [and] offers more opportunities to greater numbers of black persons than any other society, including those in Africa." Until the Biden administration, most of our military leaders agreed with Professor Patterson.

Underscoring Professor Patterson's opinion was the election of Republican Winsome Sears as Virginia's Lieutenant Governor in November 2021. During her victory speech she said, "What you are looking at is the American Dream. When I joined the Marine Corps,

I was still a Jamaican. But this country had done so much for me, I was willing, to die for it." Sears immigrated to the United States from Kingston when she was six years old in 1970. Her father arrived in New York seven years earlier with just $1.75 and took any job he could get. When she later asked him why he came to the United States during the turbulent civil rights movement he replied, "Because America is where the jobs and opportunities are."

She continued in her victory speech with an allusion to media pundits and Democrats who portray Virginia's Republican Governor-elect Glenn Youngkin as a white supremist: "There are those who want to divide us... They would like us to believe we are back in 1963 when my father came... We can live where we want. We can eat where we want... We have elected a black president – twice. Here I am. Living proof! In case you haven't noticed, I am black, and have been black all my life."

Winsome joined the Marine Corps at age 19 in 1983 where she served a three-year term as an electrician. Afterward she earned bachelor's and master's degrees from two different Virginia colleges. For a time, she also managed her own electrician business before becoming an Executive Director of a Salvation Army Women's shelter. In 2001 Sears won a seat in the Virginia House of Delegates. It was her first political victory.[22]

The remedies that Critical Race Theorists seek are a bigger problem than the Theory *per se*. They center on a redefinition of racist; one that argues that nobody can be "not racist," they can only be racist or antiracist. They lead to a society organized by quotas, something shared with radical feminism. They are antithetical to a meritocracy.

22 David Horowitz, *The Enemy Within*, 8 36, 110; Gene Dattel, *Reckoning With Race*, (New York: Encounter Books, 2017), 173; Sanford Horn, "As Leftists Cry 'White Supremacy,' a Black Republican Makes History...," *The Federalist*, (November 4, 2021): https://tinyurl.com/h5dewjx2; David Kuhn, "Exit Polls: How Obama Won," *Politico*, (November 5, 2008): https://tinyurl.com/bddc7epn; Peter Grier, "Election Results 2012: Who Won it for Obama," *Christian Science Monitor*, (November 7, 2021): https://tinyurl.com/pz9jxy9r;

CHAPTER THREE:

RADICAL FEMINISM

THERE ARE TWO REASONS that a book on Critical Race Theory and Identity Politics includes a chapter on feminism. First, feminism is a branch of Critical Theory, which might alternatively be termed Critical Gender Theory. It is based on the premise that women are victims of an oppressive patriarchy, a concept that should be debunked. Second, while nearly everyone agrees that men and women should have equal opportunities, modern radical feminism has evolved into misandry and gender preferences for women. Although only a minority of women identify with today's radical feminists, women represent more than half of America's voters. Indeed, today's Democrat Party is mostly a coalition of females and ethnic minorities.

Regarding the first point, radical feminism postulates that women are a victim class in a framework analogous to Critical Race Theory. The chief difference is that the feminists identify a governing patriarchy as their oppressor whereas CRT puts white skinned people in that role. Both feminists and CRT antiracists are increasingly gaining government and institutional endorsement to indoctrinate the imagined oppressor groups through "consciousness-raising" sessions, seminars, and lectures. Authors Robin DiAngelo and Ibram Kendi are raking in millions of dollars for such programs. Since the role of the white male is to shut up and listen, radical feminists are deaf to male disadvantages. Among them are lower life expectances and anti-male bias in divorce and child custody.

At birth females have an 81-year life expectancy compared to 75 years for males. That equates to six additional years of Social Security payments after retirement without any gender-based extra contributions to the Social Security Trust Fund. Moreover, suicide deaths by sex provide a revealing inconsistency about alleged female victimhood. While women represent 75% of the attempts, males account for 75% of the deaths. A failed suicide is a cry for help. Women tend to gain sympathy from a failed attempt whereas men more often lose the respect of others.

Although women typically complain that men are reluctant to commit to marriage, women more often initiate divorce, including over 90% of the time among college educated couples. The reasons are obvious. Women are more likely to win child custody and alimony thereby gaining monthly incomes from the ex-dad or husband. Homemakers who never held a job while married are often entitled to generous long-term, even lifetime, alimony.[1]

Due to racial preferences obtained as compensation for racism, feminists have long sought similar benefits by equating "sexism" with racism. Professor Pauline Leet originated the term in 1965 at a student-faculty forum at Franklin & Marshall College. "When you [society] argue ... that since fewer women write good poetry this justifies their total exclusion you are taking a position analogous to that of the racist—I might call you in this case a 'sexist' ... Both the racist and sexist ... are making decisions ... about someone's value by referring to factors which are in both cases irrelevant."

Leet's statement insults black Americans, whose historical disadvantages have been far more significant than those of white American women. The latter have never been slaves, nor the victims of segregation, and lynchings. Nonetheless, the radical feminist's goal is to secure a place for women on the victim scale of the alleged oppression hierarchy, thereby creating the illusion that any encounter between women and men involves a power inequality in favor of men.

Since institutional barriers to gender inequality have been in place for fifty years, today's feminists argue that the remaining barriers are invisible. Such rationalization accounts for the invention of terms like the "glass ceiling." But the expression is itself a subterfuge like 'implicit bias,' 'white privilege,' and 'systemic racism.' In each case the mere fact of a differential outcome is taken as proof of manipulation by the so-called oppressor class. David Horowitz elaborates: "Before the invention of 'sexism,' a wide variety of words were available to describe unwanted behaviors between the sexes: 'boorish,' 'inappropriate,'

---

1 Warren Farrell and John Gray, *The Boy Crisis,* (Dallas: BenBella Books, 2019), 275; Warren Farrell, *The Myth of Male Power,* (New York: Simon and Schuster, 1993), 16

'insensitive' 'offensive,' 'improper,' 'disrespectful,' and so on down a spectrum, until one reached the criminal and prosecutable, such as 'molestation,' 'assault,' and 'rape.' But once all these misbehaviors are subsumed under the rubric of 'sexism' and thus linked to 'racism,' committing any of them is easily magnified into an offense associated with discrimination, slavery, and oppression."[2]

In *The Madness of Crowds,* Douglas Murray corrects the feminist myth that all male-female interactions involve a power imbalance tilted toward men. Many women have a power that men do not. It is the ability to drive members of the opposite sex mad with sexual desire. It can make otherwise successful men destroy themselves. A young woman of only nineteen or twenty can entice a man with everything in the World, at the height of his accomplishments, to wreck himself. She can make him behave like a fool and cause him to ruin his life for a few moments of physical pleasure. Jeffrey Epstein clients are only a starting point.

Feminists lament the prevalence of anorexia nervosa among young women. Although it is indeed a regrettable disorder, it is undeniably motivated by a young woman's urge to increase her sexual power. She recognizes that a beautiful woman is a celebrity. People, especially men, turn their heads when she walks into a room.[3]

After Gretchen Carlson accused Fox News' CEO, Roger Ailes, of sexual harassment, the former Miss America won a $20 million settlement. Since she was 26 years younger than Ailes, she could have stopped his ill-mannered behavior with a slap in the face. Perhaps she instead realized that yielding to his sexual advance could make her a multimillionaire. Maybe she knew that if he did not give her a lucrative job, she could disclose his misconduct and win an easy multimillion dollar settlement. After Ailes resigned, the public judged him guilty and a group of twenty other previously silent women piled-on. He died less than a year after resigning from Fox.

A year after Carlson got her $20 million, Fox News legal analyst Lis Wiehl settled a $32 million claim against Bill O'Reilly who hosted one of the network's most popular shows. Ten years earlier she authored a

---

2 David Horowitz, *The Enemy Within*, 55-57

3 Douglas Murray, *The Madness of Crowds*, (London, Bloomsbury Continuum, 2019), 84; Warren Farrell, *The Myth of Male Power*, 13

book titled *The 51% Minority*, arguing that women remained victims even after four decades of feminist progress. O'Reilly had to pay Wiehl's settlement himself.[4]

Although feminists who complain of a gender power imbalance get the public sympathy, the casting couch has long been a tool available to women to advance their careers. While many women regret having used it, they fail to appreciate that heterosexual males generally don't even get the option. The powerful men on the couch generally want women lying there with them. Typically, the young and beautiful women can pack a latent #MeToo accusation as a parachute. Only the woman gets the parachute. If the affair becomes public, the male's career often ends ignominiously, and the lady gets a multimillion-dollar settlement. As godfather Don Corleone put it, "Men cannot make mistakes. Women and children can make mistakes, but not men." Despite feminist rhetoric to the contrary, the public is gentler toward women and more demanding of men.

Consider the Supreme Court Justice confirmation hearings for President Donald Trump's two appointees. Democrats suspected that both Brett Kavanaugh and Amy Barrett would oppose abortion, but they let the female nominee breeze through and tried to destroy Kavanaugh's reputation. At the eleventh hour they brought forth a woman with a dubious 30-year-old sexual harassment accusation against him. She could supply no witnesses. In an attempt to avoid testifying, she claimed she was afraid to fly from California. But when she ultimately did testify, she accidentally revealed that she had taken multiple long airline trips in prior years. In short, she lied. Feminists have so conditioned women into accusing white males of sexual misconduct that some will do so without hesitation, knowing they are immune to social censure particularly since the mainstream media will support them.[5]

After the corporate media learned four years ago that former Vice President Mike Pence never dines with women unless accompanied by his wife, they accused him of sexism. Instead of interpreting the practice as his way to protect himself from false sexual harassment

---

4 Emily Steel and Michael Schmidt, "Bill O'Reilly Settled New Harassment Claim …," *The New York Times,* (October 21, 2017): https://tinyurl.com/y75rn9dn

5 David Horowitz, *The Enemy Within*, 67-68

charges they instead viewed it as discrimination against professional women. They argued that it denied such women access to the Vice President in a way that did not apply to men. But among men vulnerable to false #MeToo allegations, safety measures similar to Pence's are growing. In December 2018 *Bloomberg* interviewed thirty senior financial executives. Many admitted to no longer having dinner alone with female executives. Additionally, some refused to sit next to them on airline flights. Others even insisted that their hotel rooms be booked on different floors.

The feminist press promptly complained. The *Los Angeles Times* editorialized, "If professional women and men cannot be alone together, women are the ones who will pay. They will not have the kind of mentoring that promotes workplace advancement. They will not develop the same kinds of relationships with bosses that their male colleagues do. They will lose out." A gender and psychology lecturer at UCLA added, "I believe this is gender discrimination. If you don't go out to dinner with a woman, it's hard to have a woman be your campaign manager or your chief of staff or whoever you need to regularly meet with." They gave no thought to Pence's vulnerability to female sexual predators, notwithstanding media personalities Wiehl and Carlson having won combined settlements of over $50 million.

Perhaps no woman has been a bigger beneficiary of corporate media feminists than Vice President Kamala Harris. In the early days of the Biden Administration, the press pointedly referred to the new presidency as the "Biden-Harris Administration." Even though the vice presidency has long been an impotent office, Harris whines that her role is uniquely minimized because she is a woman. Nonsense. When asked almost 200 years ago if he would consider becoming Vice President, Massachusetts Senator Daniel Webster replied, "I do not propose to be buried until I am dead."

In November 2021 a former Harris staffer told CNN, "It's hard to miss the specific energy that the White House brings to defend a white man, knowing that Kamala has spent almost a year taking a lot of the hits that the West Wing didn't want to take themselves." The remark referred to Biden's quick defense of Transportation Secretary Pete Buttigieg for irresponsibly taking paternity leave during the global supply chain crisis.

In truth, Harris has been given major opportunities and shrank from them. Most notable was Biden's request that she stop the flood of illegal immigration across the Mexican border. When she tried to dodge the responsibility, Biden forgivingly let her address it ineffectively by announcing that she would lead the Administration's talks with Mexico and Central American countries about slowing the tide of migrants at the sources of origin.

Earlier when NBC's Lester Holt asked her during an interview, "Why haven't you been to the Southern border?" she replied with a laugh and flippantly remarked: "And I haven't been to Europe [either]." Despite the characteristic attempt to avoid responsibility, people "close to Harris" were angry with Biden for failing to mount a stronger defense of Kamala over the Holt interview. While quick to fault others for her problems, Harris is unable to see how she is often out of step with America's most fundamental values. One example is a Memorial Day tweet she sent wishing Americans an enjoyable long weekend without mentioning the reason for the holiday.

Even though the sisterhood press usually pampers her, in June 2021 *Politico* reported that her office was often in chaos. One source said, "People are thrown under the bus from the very top, there are short fuses and it's an abusive environment." Despite all the pampering from Democrat Party leaders and the press, Harris can only see herself as a victim.[6]

Feminist dogma so saturates our society that the corporate media perpetually reports women as the victims of any gender-based statistic, practice, or policy. But Americans are increasingly discovering that there is something rotten about feminist arguments concerning "norms" unpracticed until the day before yesterday.

When author Douglas Murray participated on a "Women Mean Business" panel he found that the ladies had a one-sided perspective on privilege. They could readily discern it in men but could not see it in themselves. By any measure, however, the conference women were among the top percentile of wage earners, male or female, anywhere in the World. They are paid large salaries, have great contacts, and see more opportunities every month than the average male gets in a lifetime.

---

6 Lee Brown and Samuel Chamberlain, "Kamala Harris Sidelined Amid Growing Tensions With Biden," *New York Post* (November 15, 2021): https://tinyurl.com/tcwjtjda

Nonetheless, whenever the panelists spoke of privilege, they could only speak about what they imagine they *don't* have. Similarly, Facebook's Cheryl Sanders can only see the privileges she lacks compared to her boss, Mark Zuckerberg. She is evidently unaware of the privilege she holds by almost never having to take the heat when Facebook comes under fire. That job defaults to Zuckerberg. Similarly, celebrity actresses complain that male actors get better roles and demand that Hollywood change until the ladies are no longer victims. Their victim status remains a media cause célèbre even though nearly 100% of males would be delighted to have such incomes and social status.[7]

The second reason this book includes a chapter on feminism is to underscore the political connection between Critical Race Theory and feminism, resulting in Identity Politics. Feminists developed the theory of intersectionality to amplify their political power by making common cause with racial and ethnic minorities. They imagine intersectionality as a "matrix of oppression" that victimizes vulnerable groups such as women and minorities. Therefore, the interests of any intersectional group, concerns the interests of all. When such groups unite against a common foe, such as white males, they advance the interests of all intersectional groups.

Even though power-through-unification can work politically, intersectionality is inauthentic. Consider the "Women Mean Business" conference. Although many attendees benefitted from gender-based affirmative action, it's unlikely any would stand aside to let a less privileged man take her job. It's also unlikely that she would even offer her place to a member of a marginalized group of a different skin color or class. Yet young males, particularly those working for big institutions, have been stepping aside for women for more than half a century. That's how female executives such as Carly Fiorina and Marissa Mayer became the CEOs of Hewlett Packard and Yahoo!, respectively. It also explains why those companies became train wrecks. Fiorina and Mayer are classic examples of affirmative action hires who got promoted beyond their level of competence.

---

7 Douglas Murray, *The Madness of Crowds*, 86; Robin Abcarian, "Mike Pence won't dine alone with a woman," *The Los Angeles Times*, (April 5, 2017): https://tinyurl.com/2p84e97r

Fortunately, people are increasingly questioning the type of feminism that accuses America of having a rape culture because the facts don't support the claim. Consider, for example, a Yale survey dubiously reporting that 35% of female undergraduates are sexually assaulted. If parents believed the statistic, the long waiting list of female students hoping to get into the university would not exist. Unfortunately, such absurd claims show that feminists have the influence to repeatedly lie and have their lies accepted as truth by the media. A classic example is the gender pay gap.[8]

For decades feminists have stated that women are paid $0.77 for every dollar a male worker gets. The figure is derived by totaling all female wages and comparing the figure to the sum-total of all male wages. It makes no allowance for the fact that women and men tend to hold different jobs, work dissimilar hours weekly, and have different educational credentials.

According to Georgetown University's Center on Education and the Workforce men overwhelmingly outnumber women in the ten most remunerative academic majors except one. The other nine are fields in engineering, mathematics, and computer science where males represent 85% of the graduates. Consequently, only 7% of female graduates were employed in high paying computer and engineering jobs, compared to 38% of males. Conversely, the ten lowest paid academic majors are dominated by women. They include Early Childhood Education, Psychological Counselling, and Social Work. Women represent a minority in only one of the ten. In the remaining nine, they represent nearly 80%.

Even the pro-feminist Obama Administration released a paper concluding that the oft-cited 23% gender wage gap "may be almost entirely the result of individual choices being made by both male and female workers... [T]he differences in the compensation of men and women are the result of a multitude of factors and ... the raw wage gap should not be used as the basis to justify corrective action. Indeed, there may be nothing to correct."

---

8 Richard Perez-Pena, "1 in 4 Women Experience Sexual Assault on Campus," *The New York Times*, (September 21, 2015): https://tinyurl.com/3ka8txf3

In addition to the work choices noted above, men are more likely to take dangerous jobs and jobs that require long absences from home. One example is work on offshore oil drilling platforms. Not only are nearly all the laborers male, but 97% of the naval architecture and marine engineering graduates at Georgetown were also males. Similarly, in 2017 less than 3% of loggers were women, a job that paid $42,000 a year. By comparison 94% of child day care workers were female, earning average annual salaries only $24,000.

Even within the same profession, men and women make different choices that impact how much money they make. A Harvard gender gap study within a single profession showed that sexism did not cause the lower pay for women. The study involved drivers for the Massachusetts Bay Transportation Authority (MBTA).

Since the workforce was unionized, all workers in the same job were paid the same hourly amount. Promotions were strictly based on seniority. Even though there was almost no wiggle room for a sexist boss to discriminate against women, female drivers earned only $0.89 for every dollar paid to men. Several non-discriminatory factors explain the gap. Male drivers worked 83% more overtime than did females. They were also twice as likely to take overtime shifts on short notice, which paid time-and-a-half. The study authors, both women, concluded that the apparent gap could be explained entirely by the different choices that the men and women made. In short, women chose lower pay because pay was a lower priority to them than it was for men.[9]

Notwithstanding that the national gender pay gap was debunked decades ago, feminists perpetually repeat it because the corporate media treats it with authority. Consequently, feminists still use it to win concessions, such as anti-male quotas.

In November 2021 Boston's State Street Global Advisors, one of the World's largest investment managers, disclosed that employees could no longer hire white men without first obtaining permission

---

9 Mark Perry, "Bulk of Earnings Gender Gap Can be Explained ...,"*Foundation for Economic Education,* (September 6, 2021): https://tinyurl.com/9hbykxd8; John Phelan, "Gender Wage Gap: Explained Entirely By Work Choices," *Foundation for Economic Education,* (December 10, 2018): https://tinyurl.com/2nfz2hkc; Steve Tobak, "The Gender Pay Gap is a Complete Myth," *CBS,* (April 17, 2011): https://tinyurl.com/yckhnytx; Christina Hoff Sommers, "The Gender Wage Gap Myth," *American Enterprise Institute,* (February 3, 2014): https://tinyurl.com/yc2b9pah

from superiors. "This is now front and central for State Street—it's on every executive's scorecard," said Jess McNicholas, the bank's head of inclusion, diversity, and corporate citizenship in London. "All of our leaders have to demonstrate at their annual appraisals what they have done to improve female representation and the number of colleagues from ethnic-minority backgrounds." Recruiters must form panels of four or five employees, including a woman and a racial or ethnic minority, when hiring middle management staff. Executives with subpar appraisals are penalized with cuts in their annual bonuses. Companies like State Street, with 40,000 employees, are looking more like the Soviet Union than a bastion of capitalism.[10]

During Senate hearings that same month, a Biden diversity nominee for Currency Comptroller, Saule Omarova, responded to criticism about her monetary principles by accusing the senators of sexism and racism. Among the former Soviet citizen's fantasies is America's gender pay gap. Two years earlier she remarked, "Until I came to the U.S., I couldn't imagine that things like [a] gender pay gap still existed. Say what you will about [the] old USSR, there was not a gender pay gap there." After absorbing criticism for the remark, she doubled down: "I never claimed that women and men were treated absolutely equally in every facet of Soviet life. But peoples' salaries were set by the state in a gender-blind manner."[11]

In the final analysis, the decades-long assertion that women are only paid $0.77 on the dollar for the same work as men should have been rejected as myth from the beginning. If true in a capitalistic society, Adam Smith's invisible hand would have directed business owners to hire only women. If the owners could get the same productivity out of female workforce as a male workforce, and reduce their labor costs by 23%, the profit motive would cause them the hire women. A gap as large as 23% would have self-corrected as each employer competed to minimize their labor costs and thereby remain profitable.

---

10 Noirin Hegarty and Robert Watt, "No Country for White Men ...," *The Times (London)*, (November 7, 2021): https://tinyurl.com/4jd8rs56

11 Veronique de Rugy, "The Gender Gap, Paid Leave Programs and the Soviet Union," *Office of the Comptroller of Currency*, (October 18, 2021): https://tinyurl.com/2p9hkda6

Perhaps the chief reason the wage gap theory wasn't promptly rejected was because of gentlemanly indulgence among male academics during the 1960s and 70s when female professors were trying to establish Gender Studies departments. Apparently, male colleagues were more concerned with encouraging newcomer ambitions than with the truth.

Persistent lies about a gender pay gap are only one sign of the corruption in modern feminism. Feminist journals overflow with ridiculous articles forever discovering new examples of female oppression. During 2017 and 2018 three academics, James Lindsay, Helen Pluckrose, and Peter Boghossian, got fed up. They submitted hoax articles to various peer-reviewed feminist journals. Their object was to expose the madness that passed for research in "grievance studies" such as Gender Studies and Black Studies. They wanted to raise awareness about the damage that Identity Politics and Critical Theory was causing in academia.

The trio wrote twenty articles that promoted absurdities, which they felt might nevertheless get published owing to liberal use of jargon and politically correct conclusions. Although the *Wall Street Journal* disclosed the scheme in October 2018, the authors had already had four articles published and three more accepted for publication. (Six had been rejected and seven were still under review.)

Among the published articles was one arguing that male dogs routinely raped female dogs. The role of jargon is evident from the title: "Rape Culture and Queer Performativity at Urban Dog Parks," published in *Gender, Place and Culture*. The paper's fictious author, "Helen Wilson," claimed to have aggregated data documenting her thesis while observing canine sexual encounters at dog parks in Portland, Oregon. Even though "Wilson's" conclusions were unwarranted, the journal's editors were impressed by the data and jargon.

"Wilson" represented that she spent hundreds of hours in three dog parks, where she observed and tallied the times when one dog humped another. When the humping was male-on-male, owners normally intervened. "Wilson" argued that the owners were thereby acting-out their inner homophobia. Conversely, when the humping was male-on-female, owners were far less likely to stop it. "Wilson" thus argued the owners were commonly overlooking dog rape. Since the sexual assault of dogs could be minimized by keeping the male dogs on a leash, "Wilson" suggested that society should figure out how to metaphorically leash human males. Before the hoax was exposed, *Gender, Place and Culture* cited the article for special merit.

Affilia, a peer-reviewed journal of women and social work, accepted a submission that was basically a rewrite of a chapter from Hitler's *Mein Kampf*. The chief difference was that women were portrayed as the victims whereas *Mein Kampf* portrayed Hitler's followers as the victims. The article's title conveys the gobbledygook language that would win journal acceptance while simultaneously obfuscating the underlying nonsense: "Our Struggle Is My Struggle: Solidarity Feminism as an Intersectional Reply to Neoliberal and Choice Feminism."

A third article, "The Conceptual Penis as a Social Construct," was published in *Cogent Social Sciences*. By decorating nonsense with a combination of popular moral sentiments and opaque jargon the paper blamed the conceptual penis for several modern problems ranging from climate change to the raping of undeveloped land through "manspreading."[12]

Although academic feminists insist that quotas and gender-preference programs are necessary remedies to correct for traditional female victimhood, girls were never a small fraction of college students during the past sixty years. In 1960 they represented 46% of incoming freshmen. They became a distinct majority in 1975 and have remained a majority ever since. In 1980 they were 54% of freshmen; 57% in the year 2000 and presently 60%. In 2020 colleges enrolled 1.5 million fewer students than in 2015 and 70% of the drop was among males. Nonetheless, due to entrenched feminist influence Americans shrug their shoulders at the long-term decline of males as a fraction of college graduates. Schools don't want to provide affirmative action for white males because they are *perceived* as privileged.

12 Andy Ngo, "Men Behind the Conceptual Penis Hoax ...," *The College Fix,* (May 22, 2017): https://tinyurl.com/2p96e82t; Robby Soave, "Anti-PC Writers Trick Seven Academic Journals into Accepting Hoax Papers...," *Reason*, (October 3, 2018): https://tinyurl.com/329fp45b

There is also little thought given to the demeaning treatment colleges heap upon freshmen males in the form of sexual assault warnings and impossible dating regulations. Girls, for example, still want boys to initiate physical contact, but also demand the right to instantly condemn any boy who makes such contact. Some will even attempt to get him expelled or convicted of sexual assault. So dominant is the feminist perspective on campus, that articles attempting to focus on the needs of boys are offset by those complaining that the declining percentage of males is chiefly unfair to women because it shrinks the pool of datable men.[13]

One example of the feminist females-are-always victims absurdity concerns the Chinese cultural preference for sons over daughters. It does not reflect an intrinsic preference for boys. Instead, it reflects a natural parental desire for financial security. Chinese tradition holds that a daughter belongs to her husband's family after she is married. Thus, she will have no responsibility to take care of her parents in their old age. Conversely, the culture holds the son accountable for the well-being of aging parents. Even if a male-baby preference is not beneficial for the entire Chinese society it is still a rational preference for the parents, particularly considering the government's one-child policy and the paucity of pensions.[14]

By corrupting gender relations modern feminism has devastated the family, the fundamental purpose of gender relations for ages. Along with Identity Politics it is also weakening the traditionally male role of defending the tribe by debasing our military.

---

13 Derek Thompson, "Colleges Have a Guy Problem," *The Atlantic*, (September 14, 2021): https://tinyurl.com/eb4ehay4; National Center for Educational Statistics: https://tinyurl.com/5aty5r56

14 Wikipedia, "Son Preference in China,": https://tinyurl.com/2p8698pw

CHAPTER FOUR:

CORRUPTED MILITARY

SHORTLY AFTER BARACK OBAMA moved into the White House in 2009, he directed the military to prepare a unified plan to promote "diversity." The result was the Military Leadership Diversity Commission, which released its final report on March 15, 2011. On that date it became clear that diversity was a euphemism for quota-driven changes in favor of blacks, women, and ethnic minorities. Although the word "quota" appears nowhere in the document, the report instead states that obtaining diversity among those of recruiting age "requires more than affirmative action." It also repeatedly emphasizes goals centered on equality of outcomes rather than equality of individual opportunity.

The commission's first goal was to get the services to "systematically develop a demographically diverse leadership that reflects the public it serves." Although the commission confessed that the services had long led the way in providing opportunities for minorities and women it added that, "[They] have not yet succeeded in developing a continuing stream of leaders who are demographically as diverse as the nation they serve."

The goal of proportionality in outcome groups (e.g., Marine Corps Sergeant Majors) is particularly difficult when applied to blacks. In 2009, blacks represented 15% of America's recruiting age population between seventeen and twenty-nine. After eligibility filters, such as no children, weight limits, and aptitude testing, sixty percent failed to qualify for enlistment. Thus, black eligibility dropped from 15% to 6%. Aptitude testing was the single biggest hurdle, representing most of the nine-point drop. The results were nearly identical when applied to the recruiting pool for Marine Corps officers. Nonetheless, blacks represent 8.6% of officers, which is comparable to their 9.0% of the population with a college degree, as required by for all officers.

One of the supposed reasons for seeking demographic diversity was to insure harmony in the Armed Services. The report quoted one general: "If you [leaders] cannot create harmony ... across coalition and national lines and across civilian/military lines, you really need to go home because your leadership is ... obsolete." As shall be explained, however, the teachings of Critical Race Theory, radical feminism, and Identity Politics in the services now—ten years after the report—is promoting dissatisfaction and resentment. Consequently, black, and female service members are taught they are victims of whites and males, respectively. Simultaneously, they are enabled to evade personal responsibility by suggesting that their failures are due to external manipulations by the oppressor class. Under such circumstances, the services can no longer be a meritocracy. Given a quota system, which is increasingly becoming the unspoken method of obtaining diversity, the best pilots may not fly our airplanes, nor the best cyber experts defend our computer networks.

Finally, the report concedes that the military had already targeted ethnic minorities and women with special recruiting efforts. For years they had been operating offices devoted to recruiting minority groups. They had regularly advertised in student newspapers at historically black colleges and prepared marketing materials especially for such institutions. They also advertised in black-centric media such as Black Entertainment Television, *The Black Collegian,* and *The Root.* The military academies promote summer seminars and candidate-parent weekend visits, targeting minority high schools. They also use preparatory schools and related programs designed to increase the pool of eligible minority and female applicants. But those efforts failed to achieve the desired diversity results.[1]

During the forty years between 1973 and 2013, the percentage of military members from the South increased from 35% to 43% whereas the fraction for all other regions of the country combined declined from 65% to 57%. The South is the only region that contributed more than its proportional share of population. Southerners have a long tradition as a warrior class, that the Biden-era military seeks to minimize. That may be one reason the services have banned displays of Confederate symbols. In defense of that culture former Navy

---

1 Military Leadership Diversity Commission, "From Representation to Inclusion: Diversity Leadership During the 21st Century," (March 15, 2011), xii-xiv, 11, 48, 53-54

Secretary and Virginia Senator Jim Webb wrote, "When you see other cultures having strengths that don't require you to go out and get your butt shot off, this particular [Southern] culture seems thankless and a kind of a curse, but it's there."[2]

Undoubtedly, President Biden's obsession with Identity Politics Left him inattentive to planning a successful military withdrawal from Afghanistan. Probably nobody at this writing can recall a more shameful performance by an American commander in chief. Regrettably, the debacle also revealed our military leadership to be infected by the same disease.

Defense Secretary Lloyd Austin and Chairman of Biden's Joint Chiefs of Staff General Mark Milley were also distracted by diversity, equity, and inclusion programs. As noted, both underscored their support for DEI at various congressional hearings. Some were as late as two months before the desperate videos of evacuees hanging on from the outside of ascending transport airplanes at the Kabul airport got into the media. Austin even promised to "root out racists and [domestic] extremists" from America's military as if their numbers were anything more than trivial. Among America's 330 million residents, for example, the Antidefamation League estimates there are only about 3,000 KKK members.[3]

When appearing before the House Appropriations Committee in June 2021 General Milley took questions from Florida Congressman Michael Waltz, a former Green Beret. Concerning questions about the teachings of Critical Race Theory at West Point, the General responded: "I've read Mao Tse-tung. I've read Karl Marx. I've read Lenin. That doesn't make me a communist... I personally find it offensive that we are accusing the United States military ... of being quote 'woke' or something else because we're studying some theories that are out there."

---

2 Department of Defense, *Population Representation of the Military Services, Fiscal Year 2013,*20, 50: https://tinyurl.com/2p9cn9ze

3 David Horowitz, *The Enemy Within,* 25; Sean Braswell, "Why the U.S. Military is so Southern," *OZY,* (November 19, 2016): https://tinyurl.com/ynjf32sp; Alex Ward, "The Pentagon is Taking a Major Step to Deal with Diversity," *Vox,* (February 12, 2021): https://tinyurl.com/2p84xyh8

Milley's answer was dismissive, not responsive. The congressman did not imply that the academy should avoid studying Left-Wing racial theories. He was objecting to apparent indoctrination, not discussion, after a cadet's family notified him of the "Understanding Whiteness and White Rage" lecture that the cadet felt had crossed the line between discussion and propaganda. The lady giving the lecture described the Republican Party platform as a platform of white supremacy. Moreover, the general's analogies are absurd. Unlike Critical Race Theorists, West Point is not inviting Maoists to give unrebutted lectures. The public is entitled to know whether the actual Army CRT lectures have been open discussions or indoctrinations. Milley's response was an attempt to preempt such questions.[4]

As a subordinate to the Secretary of Defense, Milley's remarks may have been an echo of Lloyd Austin's opinions. When testifying before the same committee, Austin said: "We do not teach critical race theory. We don't embrace critical race theory, and I think that's a spurious conversation. We are focused on extremist behaviors and not ideology—not people's thoughts, not people's political orientation. Behaviors are what we're focused on."

To the contrary, Austin does indeed seem to be focused on controlling thoughts as opposed to actions. During the past three years the Marine Corps found only sixteen cases of extremism, and most were merely social media postings. Additionally, correspondence between Congressman Waltz and West Point's Superintendent confirms that Critical Race Theory is truly included in the syllabus of at least one class and that Richard Delgado's *Critical Race Theory: An Introduction* is included among the readings.

When another congressman explained that several military members told him that CRT was being taught as indoctrination, not rebuttable theory, Austin replied dismissively, "Thanks for your anecdotal input, but I would say that I have gotten 10 times that

---

4 Congressman Michael Waltz, "Waltz Presses Austin on CRT," Press Release, (June 23, 2021): https://tinyurl.com/mrxzt48x

Ramesh Ponnuru, "Stop Lauding General Milley's Evasions on CRT," *Bloomberg,* (June 29, 2021): https://tinyurl.com/yckm2arm

amount of input, 50 times that amount, on the other side that have said, 'Hey, we're glad to have had the ability to have a conversation with ourselves and with our leadership.'"[5]

In April 2021 Congressman Waltz wrote the West Point superintendent about his concerns, most of which have proven to be valid. He learned of "workshops" at the Point with titles such as "White Power at West Point" and "Racist Dog Whistles at West Point." In September 2020 the entire Corps of Cadets watched a panel discussion in which an active-duty officer described how she awakened to her white privilege and felt guilty about the advantages she enjoyed. She also described white police officers as murderers. Waltz concluded: "These critical race theory teachings pit cadets against one another through divisive indoctrination... Unfortunately, these seminars [suggest to] our future military leaders that they should treat fellow officers and soldiers differently based on race... I cannot think of a notion more destructive to unit cohesion and morale."[6]

Shortly after Lieutenant Colonel Matthew Lohmeier published *Irresistible Revolution: Marxism's Goal of Conquest and the Unmaking of the American Military* in the spring of 2021, he was relieved of duty. Formerly the commander of the Eleventh Space Warning Squadron, his book was prompted by Secretary Austin's February 2021 instructions to "root out" extremism and racism in the military. Lohmeier found extremism, but at the opposite end of the political spectrum. The Lieutenant Colonel also noticed that directives from Austin's Defense Department suggested a witch hunt for white extremism. "Tragically, too many of our young service members are beginning to believe that [service in a white supremacist military] is precisely what they have signed up to do—not because it's true, but because it is what they are being taught."

Shortly after the February directive, Lohmeier learned that new reporting procedures for disciplinary actions required the race and gender of each person, including those who write-up the report and those who receive it. Lohmeier concluded that nature-of-infraction

---

5 Tom Bowman, "The Military Confronts Extremism," *NPR*, (April 7, 2021): https://tinyurl.com/7vffz36f; Danielle Kurtzleben, "Top General Defends Studying CRT," *NPR*, (June 23, 2021): https://tinyurl.com/mt3n2fra

6 Congressman Mike Waltz, "Waltz Requests Critical Race Theory Materials from West Point," Press Release, (April 8, 2021): https://tinyurl.com/46tjv4ra

was immaterial by comparison. In his analysis, CRT narratives are filtering down from the top military brass that suggest whites are racist even if they don't know it. They also imply that America was founded by racists, has always been racist, and is based on a constitution that codified white supremacy. The propaganda concludes that America must transform into something radically different than it ever was.

Lohmeier cited examples from personal experiences including exit interviews from those who resigned. One Asian American fed up with Identity Politics concluded the services were only interested in making more opportunities for blacks. A newly minted Air Force Academy graduate was tired of constant teachings that one's skin color determines whether he is racist, regardless of his behavior. Another non-white female planned to resign because she concluded she was assigned good opportunities only because of her skin color. Yet another non-white female explained that she was despondent that her unit's Chaplin taught that white people were "out to get her."

When Lohmeier queried officers in other service branches, he heard similar stories. He learned of black West Point cadets that grew doubtful they could take the required enlistment oath because they were unsure if they could force themselves to defend a racist country. One Air Force Academy cadet confided that "the Academy is the last place on Earth you want to be if you are a white, male, Christian." One enlistment advisor reported that high school students were losing interest in military service. Many stated that they were no longer confident about the meaning of America.[7]

Some Leftist movements that started decades ago are presently being reprised in military versions. In 1962 the Students for a Democratic Society (SDS) gathered at a conference in Port Huron, Michigan where it issued its "Port Huron Statement" calling for the American republic to be replaced by a "participatory democracy" in which the rulers needed only a bare majority to control of the national government. The statement accused the United States of failing to achieve international peace and economic justice. It urged the federal government to "invest" more in welfare and rejected the widespread anticommunist sentiment of the Cold War.

---

7 Lt. Col. Matthew Lohmeier, *Irresistible Revolution: Marxism's Goal of Conquest & The Unmaking of the American Military,* (Self Published, 2021), 130-34

After it became clear that America was not going to evolve in that manner, the SDS cozied-up to totalitarian communist states like Cuba and North Vietnam. Before the SDS faded away it sent forth spokesmen like Bill Ayers who pledged war against America and went underground to lead a terrorist's cult. Although the SDS and the Port Huron Statement never amounted to much, they inspired a group of 2020 West Point seniors to prepare a manifesto of their own.

One section of the West Point Manifesto complained that the academy failed to teach antiracism. The signatories grumbled that they graduated without understanding they were still racist, could not identify microaggressions, did not appreciate their white privilege, and only realized at graduation that America is a white supremacy country. Among the signatories were valedictorians, Fulbright Scholars, a Rhodes Scholar, a class president, and captains of various sports teams. The class president warned that the Point "will fail every member of the Army" if it does not become determinedly antiracist. Specific complaints and predictions fall into the CRT narrative such as: "[America was] founded and built upon white supremacy;" it is saturated with "intersectional discriminations, microaggressions, and implicit biases; its leaders are complicit because they only pretend to care about blacks."

The 2021 National Defense Authorization Act promoted an agenda full of CRT tenets. Equality of opportunity is ignored and replaced with a new diversity vision emphasizing equality of outcomes. The goal is not to treat everybody the same. Instead, the objective is to ensure that all races, sexes, and ethnic groups get a proportional share of the leadership and other valued jobs.

It implies the Air Force should strive to have a proportional share of women pilots. How that is to be accomplished without unnecessary risks should the women fail to match the performance of the males they replace is never explained. The bill's House version would have appointed numerous high level Chief Diversity Officers to approve promotions only for candidates who subscribe to Critical Race Theory and fit the desired race and gender characteristics. It also calls for the swift removal of so-called racist monuments, without providing a clear description of the term "racist."

When President Donald Trump learned late in his term that CRT was taught in many federal agencies and within the military, he issued an executive order to stop it. The order was only in force four months because President Biden revoked it. While it was operative Lieutenant Colonel Lohmeier observed that *ad hoc* groups within the military circumvented its prohibitions. He attended one such discussion led by a black female in October 2020. Her group had invited everyone on his base despite Trump's prohibitions. The applicable textbook was Ijeoma Oluo's *So You Want to Talk About Race.*

The book's "Discussion Guide" states, "the comfort of white attendees should be very, very far down on the priority list." If whites "feel strongly that they need to center their feelings and experiences in the discussion, [the group leader] should set up a space away from the group where they can talk with other white people. Do not let it take over the discussion or become a burden that people of color in the group must bear." Predictably, it teaches that America is "a white supremacist society [that must] be dismantled piece by piece." It warns that any speech that makes non-whites "feel unsafe" is "an act of violence," thereby defining mere words as violence. Conversely, if group discussions make whites feel uncomfortable it advises, "do not allow [them] to be treated as if harm had been done to them."[8]

The year 2020 brought similar developments to the Air Force Academy. In July a Colorado Springs newspaper headlined an article, "Air Force football takes firm social stance with video in support of Black Lives Matter." The team posted a three-minute video on its Facebook page in which the team and its coaches claim that "black lives are not treated as equal in our society." One coach borrowed CRT themes when he explained that it is not enough to be "not racist." Another coach followed with the predictable argument that it is necessary to be "antiracist." A white coach said, "It is time to recognize my bias." The head coach personally endorsed Black Lives Matter.

After Air Force Academy alumni saw the video, some organized a group to have it removed. Following hundreds of email exchanges with academy officers, team coaches, and Air Force brass, they got nothing but resistance. In September 2020 they officially filed a lawsuit to have it taken down. Their attorney, Michael Rose, was well known as an opponent of discriminatory practices in the military over the past fifty

---

8 Lt. Col. Matthew Lohmeier, *Irresistible Revolution*, 111-15, 138-41

years. His filing linked Black Lives Matter to Marxism. He correctly added that much of the language in the video had been prohibited by President Trump's 13950 Executive Order.

Two months later—after the November presidential election—the Inspector General (IG) replied. His letter opined that nothing in the video was a violation of Air Force Instructions, Defense Department Directives, or even the 13950 Executive Order. Consequently, the IG dismissed the complaint. He also cited a July 2020 Justice Department memorandum stating that the Black Lives Matter Global Network is "not ... a partisan political group."[9]

One of Lohmeier's most alarming conclusions is that American military leaders are lenient toward provocative actions, outspoken remarks, and controversial social media posts by service members that support a "woke" agenda, but simultaneously intolerant of anyone who supports traditional values. Among the examples he cites concerns two Naval Academy Cadets at opposing ends of the political spectrum.

One, a white male, posted on Twitter that the looters and rioters in the summer of 2020 should be met with force. Another, a black female, tweeted about riots then in progress in Kentucky, "I hope they burn down the entire city of Louisville." The white male was forced to leave the Naval Academy whereas Lohmeier could find no reprimand against the black female. The white male had to go to court where a judge ruled that his rights of due process had been violated but gave no immediate relief. Instead, the cadet reached a settlement that enabled him to graduate after ten weeks of sensitivity training.[10]

Rather than focus on military threats from such countries as China and Russia as well as international terrorists, General Milley's Army is exterminating all Confederate names and symbols. In 2020 Congress passed the National Defense Authorization Act over President Trump's veto. He vetoed the bill because it requires the re-naming of ten Army bases named in honor of Confederate veterans. A year after enactment, the Naming Commission Chairperson revealed that they had received 27,000 new name suggestions. Among them were many "quite intense" proposals objecting to the renaming. "There are some folks who are distinctly opposed [to renaming bases named for Confederates] and

---

9 Lt. Col. Matthew Lohmeier, *Irresistible Revolution*, 143-45

10 Lt. Col. Matthew Lohmeier, *Irresistible Revolution*, 146-52

the verbiage they used is quite deliberate," said Michelle Howard, the retired Navy admiral and chairwoman of the commission. "They make it clear that they do not support the commission."

She added that the renaming process would also apply to military assets for other services beyond the Army. Her commission will submit the names by October 2022. Congress will then instruct the defense secretary to change the names of bases, ships, buildings, and other military assets that commemorate the Confederacy. She also added that there were even thousands of additional named items across the military that likely qualified to be changed.[11]

In 2021 the Navy launched an "oiler" named for Harvey Milk who was the first openly gay man elected to public office when he joined the San Francisco Board of Supervisors in 1977. Although Milk is commonly portrayed as a gay rights pioneer, several critics have accused him of multiple homosexual relationships with underage boys. Among the alleged victims was 16-year-old Jack McKinley who met Milk in 1963 when the latter was 33 years old. Even Randy Shilts, a Milk hagiographer, concedes the relationship. McKinley eventually committed suicide. Another alleged example was Gerald Dols who stated in a 2008 radio interview that Milk convinced him to run away from his Minnesota family to join Milk in San Francisco. According to Dols, Milk told the boy, "Don't tell your parents." When the parents learned the facts of their son's disappearance, they filed a complaint with Minnesota's attorney general.[12]

Senators and congressmen who voted for the base renaming commission during the 2020 race riots may wish to reconsider the banishment of Confederate symbols. Only the zeitgeist of that period enabled a vocal minority to demonize the Confederate soldier, much like the many Americans who sneered at returning Vietnam veterans in the 1960s and 70s. Today most Americans old enough to remember cringe with shame when recalling such incidents.

---

11 Corey Dickstein, "Quite Intense: Public Offers 27,000 Suggestions . . .," *Stars and Stripes,* (October 1, 2021): https://tinyurl.com/2p966zw4

12 "Woke U.S. Navy Names Ship After Accused pedophile, Harvey Milk," *The Post Millennial,* (November 8, 2021): https://tinyurl.com/2p89eyu9

We should be aware that decisions to tear down century-old monuments put us at risk for future remorse. Dishonoring such monuments demeans later generations of American warriors who were inspired by the Confederate soldier. Consider, for example, that post-Civil-War Southerners consistently came to our nation's defense more readily than did other Americans. Even presently, 44% of America's military are from the South notwithstanding the region's lower 36% share of the nation's population.

During World War II, the first American flag to fly over the captured Japanese fortress at Okinawa was a Confederate battle flag. It was put there by a group of marines to honor their company commander. He happened to be a South Carolinian who suffered a paralyzing wound during the mopping up process. Some of the tank crews that freed prisoners from German concentration camps also flew that flag.

The academic community leads those wanting to remove Confederate statues, which they characterize as racist. In doing so they violate the American Historical Society's warning against presentism, which is defined as an uncritical tendency to interpret the past in terms of modern values. It fails to recognize that racial attitudes throughout America 150 years ago were different than they are today.

Eventually, toppling Confederate statues evolved into a mob sport, with impunity for the vandals. Since such conduct requires no more bravery than kicking a puppy, we may wonder what comes next. New York City removed a nearly two-hundred-year-old statue of Thomas Jefferson late in 2021. Anti-statue activists are behaving much like the leaders of the former Soviet Union where censorship and rewritten history was part of the state's effort to ensure that the correct political spin was put on their history. In response, George Orwell warned, "The most effective way to destroy a people is to deny and obliterate their own understanding of their history."

Finally, in hearings at the Armed Services Committee senators began pressing General Milley on the cost of initiatives concerning alleged white nationalism within the military. They questioned whether such a witch hunt should be prioritized over sustaining the services as a lethal fighting force. Twelve Republicans sent him letter complaining that the Department of Defense was more focused on including Critical Race Theory indoctrination than in recruiting personnel and training them for combat. Regarding Milley's obsession to excise white supremacists and domestic extremists from the services the senators wrote, "All this is taking place despite clear data that pegs the number of extremists in our military as miniscule."[13]

The American white supremacist is a phantom. According to a 2019 study by Pew Research only 15% of white Americans consider being white as very important to their identity. In contrast, 74% of blacks say their racial identity is very important to them. The comparable percentages for Hispanics and Asians living in America is 59%. Blacks uniquely stand out as being most obsessed with race and whites as uniquely indifferent. But, as the next chapter explains, our country's elite is censoring information to convince Americans of just the opposite. In truth, Black Lives Matter and Antifa are existential threats, not white supremacy.[14]

13 Caroline Vakil, "Republicans Press Milley ...," *The Hill,* (November 4, 2021): https://tinyurl.com/4sd49unj

14 Juliana Horowitz, Anna Brown, Kiana Cox, "The Role of Race and Ethnicity in Americans' Personal Lives," *Pew Research Center,* (April 9, 2019): https://tinyurl.com/yw8h5xed

CHAPTER FIVE:

BIG TECH

THE BIG CONSUMER-FACING technology companies on the West Coast, such as Amazon, Microsoft, Apple, Twitter, Facebook, Netflix, and Google-YouTube, have become the censorship arm of the Democrat Party. Of the seventeen tech companies valued at more than $100 billion, all but the employees of one gave more political donations to Democrats than Republicans. Netflix showed the most asymmetry with 98% slated for Democrats, but even the venerable IBM's contributions were a lopsided 90% for Democrats. Except for Twitter, which was below the $100 billion market value threshold, employees of the companies above gave an arithmetic average of 85% to Democrats and 15% to Republicans.[1]

Given such a propensity for Democrats it's not surprising that Big Tech companies use their power to influence election outcomes. One of the most egregious examples was Twitter's censorship of the *New York Post,* a 220-year-old newspaper. Less than a month before the November 2020 presidential election the *Post* revealed that an abandoned laptop computer of Joe Biden's son, Hunter, carried evidence that he peddled influence while his father served as Vice President. Yet most of the remaining mainstream media ignored the story. Twitter and Facebook quickly blocked the story on their platforms, squelching vital information even as America's early voters were casting their ballots. Big Tech and Big Media got their way, at the expense of our democracy. Under such influence taxpayer funded National Public Radio refused to carry the story, which it erroneously termed "discredited," and Public Television's evening news treated the story dismissively.

---

1 Ari Levy, "The most liberal and conservative tech companies ranked by employees' political donations," *CNBC,* (July 2, 2020): https://tinyurl.com/59erjv8j

After his dad was safely embedded in the White House and the FBI had possession of the laptop, Hunter finally admitted that the computer was his. Data show that in the days following the *Post's* October 2020 article, public Google searchers for instructions on how to change an early vote ballot spiked. Even though the leading social media sites tried to censor the news, many Americans learned of it anyway. Big Tech was never penalized for its censorship and continues to censor in favor of Democrats. As late as the summer of 2021, YouTube blocked videos accurately predicting that President Biden would attempt to impose vaccine mandates. Earlier that year YouTube restricted videos suggesting that COVID-19 might have originated in a Chinese laboratory, which they dismissed as a conspiracy theory.[2]

In the same month the *Post* broke the Hunter Biden laptop story, a Facebook whistleblower contacted Missouri Senator Josh Hawley. The Senator was curious to know why Facebook and Twitter almost simultaneously decided to censor the *Post's* story. Even though the director of national intelligence confirmed publicly that American agencies had learned that the laptop's information was not foreign disinformation but authentically Hunter's, Facebook and Twitter continued to suppress the story. When federal prosecutors announced in December (after Joe Biden was President-elect) that Hunter was under criminal investigation, Facebook and Twitter refused to answer questions about how they decided to censor the original story, apparently in tandem.

By November 2020 Senator Hawley was convinced of the whistleblower's authenticity. His documents revealed that Facebook was deep into the censorship business. The company's ability to monitor what users were saying and doing was beyond anything that had yet been disclosed. Moreover, the senator learned that Facebook did not censor by itself, Big Tech platforms coordinated their efforts.

Hawley concluded that Big Tech was more than a collection of monopolies; it was a *movement* he compared to the Robber Barons of the Gilded Age. The modern day oligopolists have similar objectives. Their aim is to build a more connected and global community. They want society to mirror the politically progressive convictions of the

---

2 The Editorial Board, "One year later, *The Post's* Hunter Biden Reporting is Vindicated," *New York Post,* (October 12, 2021): https://tinyurl.com/bdh8m9kb

Democrat Party, a World with no borders. If the goal requires that America be fundamentally changed to fuel Big Tech financial growth, so be it. They are prepared to use their powers to change society by changing America's traditional principles, morals, and values.

Amazon, Facebook, Twitter, Google-YouTube, and Netflix are among those who realize that America will eventually be only a small part of their corporate revenues. China's population is over three times bigger than America's. Even if her per capita income becomes only one third as large as ours, her market will be bigger than America's. Similarly, Amazon can probably make more money selling washing machines made in China where labor costs are lower, than those manufactured in the Whirlpool plants at Benton Harbor, Michigan.

The whistleblower, pseudonymed "Mike Gilgan", disclosed that Facebook did not censor with mere algorithms. Some of the most sensitive censorship involved real people. By utilizing a corroboration tool termed Tasks—basically an online forum—they worked across various moderation teams. A participant wanting to censor a website might start a thread, "Ban this URL (Universal Resource Locator)." Censorship decisions would ultimately be reached through online discussions, which might include senior management.

Many URLs targeted by Facebook censors were politically conservative websites and individuals. As so-called fact checking sources, Facebook relies upon Left-leaning websites like the Southern Poverty Law Center. "Gilgan" reported that Facebook's internal platforms are dominated by Far-Left content. He also claims Facebook consults with Twitter and Google regularly when deciding to ban individuals and websites.[3]

Senator Hawley summarized: "'Gilgan's' revelations were shocking. They disclosed a company rife with political bias and arrogant with power. Facebook mouthed platitudes about user privacy and choice; company executives disclaimed any political manipulation or unequal treatment; but the truth was clearly otherwise. Facebook had a political agenda, or more precisely, a social agenda, and was determined to use its power to achieve it. User privacy and data security were treated as niceties to be rehearsed in public and then ignored."

---

3 Josh Hawley, *The Tyranny of Big Tech*, (Washington, D.C.: Regnery Publishing, 2021), 90-92

When the Senate Judiciary Committee voted to invite Twitter and Facebook CEOs to testify online in November 2020 about the *Post* incident, the vote was strictly along party lines. Not one Democrat objected that the two companies had effectively censored a venerable newspaper. To the contrary, Democrats were delighted that Twitter and Facebook suppressed news detrimental to their Party's presidential candidate. Discovering the truth was a lower priority than protecting their political power.

Given "Gilgan's" information, Committee interrogation by Hawley and others enabled the senator to realize that Big Tech censors were determined to enforce the viewpoints of the social, political, and cultural bias of their class, meaning the high earning, coastally enclaved liberals committed to a global economy with little border interference.

Facebook's so-called news curators intervened to squelch stories such as the Obama-era IRS targeting of conservatives. When politically conservative websites broke a story, Facebook "curators" interfered to find the same story on a Left-Wing website and raise the profile of the latter at the expense of the former. One former curator remarked that Facebook once got a lot of pressure for its shortage of Black Lives Matter stories. As a result, management boosted BLM stories in the ordering. Stories "injected" into the "trending news" module had a better probability of becoming popular Facebook news items. According to Senator Hawley, "None of this was remotely surprising given the background of the curators ... they were a set of young journalists educated largely at elite universities. They were merely imposing the preferences of their social class."[4]

Like other Facebook employees the curators were likely of the same social class as the Simon and Schuster editors who persuaded their employer to renege on its commitment to publish Hawley's *Tyranny of Big Tech*, which was eventually released by another publisher. That twenty-something-aged editors could have such power at a publisher as old as Simon and Schuster is pathetic. Young editors at a traditional New York publisher should be grateful for the privilege of working there. The inflated egos of those not yet experienced to know much of anything should not be allowed to veto corporate commitments on

4 Josh Hawley, *The Tyranny of Big Tech*, 94-95, 97-99

a whim. Simon and Schuster should realize that there's a long list of youthful editors, probably from the same schools, that would eagerly take the place of those who censored Senator Hawley.

Google's employees were so distraught over Hillary Clinton's 2016 presidential election defeat, that the management team convened a company-wide sympathy session. Although Google denies they manipulated search engine results to favor Hillary, psychologist Roger Epstein had been researching such capabilities since two years earlier. Initially he focused on the placement of news articles and other links provided to users after a Google search query. Even before Hillary lost, Epstein reported that he could alter the undecided vote by more than 12% merely by controlling the order of Google's search results, with those at the top having the most influence.

In the months leading up to the Trump-Clinton election Epstein studied more than 13,000 election-specific searches on three different engines. He found a distinct Hillary bias in Google's searches. She dominated the top ten listing on the first page. Epstein concluded that Google's search algorithm moved 2.6 million undecided voters toward Clinton, which was over 85% of her popular vote margin. It happened again in 2018 when Epstein decided that the Google engine displayed a strong political bias toward the Democrat Party.

But search results *per se*, were not Google's only tool. The search window has an autocomplete function that suggests search terms the moment the user begins to type. Epstein found that the autocomplete function had a powerful effect on undecided and uninformed voters. His results suggested that autocomplete could nudge a fifty-fifty split among undecided voters to as much as a ninety-to-ten landslide in favor of the politics associated with the autocomplete terms. All of this happened without the knowledge of the user. By October 2017, four of the first five autocomplete suggestions for Donald Trump were negative.

Finally, Google had a third way to spread its influence. Specifically, its various advertising networks such as DoubleClick and AdSense placed ads on third party websites, classically online versions of newspapers and magazines. In spring 2020 Google started threatening to remove politically conservative websites from the Google network if the websites failed to make various changes. Among such concessions included revising their news sources and eliminating reader comment sections.

In one case, Google threatened to remove *The Federalist* from its online ad network after NBC News complained to Google about news reporting at *The Federalist*. Instead of banning *The Federalist*, Google required that it aggressively monitor its reader comments to censor objectionable remarks, a chore that Google-owned YouTube said was too big for them to do for their own viewers. Since it was also an unwieldy job for *The Federalist*, they appeased Google by removing the reader comments section entirely.[5]

Through its ownership of various subsidiaries, especially YouTube, Google has evolved into something more than the dominant search engine. It is a 21st century version of a newspaper, television station, and radio channel all in one. Google's algorithms *make* the news, and its censorship defines the Overton Window of acceptable topics. It is the latter that appeals mostly to the Left. As they see it the problem is not that Big Tech sets the boundaries of Overton Window but that they don't censor enough to further narrow it. By their lights Big Tech has failed to use its power over information to deliberately advance the progressive agenda. Google dropped its once famous "Don't be evil" motto in 2018 because it no longer saw itself as a change agent. Instead, it became an advocate of a status quo in which society is managed by the cultural elite.

Aside from wanting open borders to promote a global economy, Google and Big Tech want the freedom to shift their profits from one jurisdiction to another. All shifts are done electronically, meaning fictively, until they land on the one with the lowest rates. By one estimate, Amazon, Facebook, Google, Apple, and Microsoft avoided over $100 billion in taxes during the last ten years. Amazon paid almost none. This has led to an unholy alliance between Big Tech and Big Banks. The latter are overly focused on mere paper-shuffling activities to avoid taxes for themselves and clients.[6]

The monopolistic armor of Facebook, Google-YouTube, Twitter, and Amazon owes much to favorable provisions of the omnibus 1996 Telecommunications Act. Specifically, Section 230 of the 1996 Communications Decency Act exempts consumer-facing Internet companies from liability for the libelous actions of their users. Thus, the

---

5 Josh Hawley, *The Tyranny of Big Tech*, 100-102
6 Josh Hawley, *The Tyranny of Big Tech*, 104, 109, 112-114, 116

Act prevents third party victims of any posts by users of the platforms from collecting libel damages from the parent companies. Victims must instead seek redress from the applicable users who made the posts. Often such users are careless Internet addicts without enough money to provide satisfaction to victims even when the victims win a judgment. If the Act instead enabled victims to win judgements from the operators of the platforms, Twitter, Facebook, YouTube and the others would likely have been bankrupted by such lawsuits years ago.

Although the 1996 Congress intended to promote commercial growth for Internet platforms by granting them a liability exemption for the behavior of reckless users, it also wanted to halt the spread of pornography. Consequently, Section 230 gave the Internet platform authority to edit user content without transforming itself into a publisher. This was a crucial distinction because publishers, such as newspapers, are indeed subject to libel claims. The Section also stipulated that any Internet platform that entirely removes content— as might be mandated by anti-obscenity statutes—will avoid liability if it acts in "good faith." Congress expected that edits and removals would be chiefly applied against obscenity.

Barely a year later, however, the Supreme Court eliminated the requirement to remove obscenity as unconstitutional. But Big Tech wanted more. They wanted the freedom to edit and censor user-generated content without being held to "good faith" efforts of fairness. They won such freedom through a series of court rulings. Consequently, by 2016 they were routinely editing and censoring content that supported politically conservative viewpoints because most of their employees favored Far-Left viewpoints. Such is not "good faith" censorship.

The liberalization of Section 230 has been incalculably valuable to Big Tech. It gives them free access to the user-generated content needed to construct media platforms where they can entice advertisers to run ads and through which they can sell merchandise. Thanks to the court-redrafted Section 230, however, they need produce no media programing but can control everything. *Users* produce the content, which Big Tech tweaks for optimal consumer engagement via algorithms. Presently Big Tech has all the power to control the flow of information with none of the common law responsibility required of any other corporate actor.

Court rulings have so distorted Section 230's intent that it has been transformed from a regulation to control Big Tech into a shield to protect it from competition. Google-YouTube, Facebook, and Twitter are multimedia publishers having no obligation to pay contributors while enjoying the freedom to monetize the work-product of most contributors through advertisements and online product sales.[7]

In the late 1990s it became evident that Google had developed a tool that would become the Internet's most popular search engine. Even though they consistently gained market share on competitors such as Yahoo! and Altavista, they had no way of making money until becoming acquainted with Berkeley's Hal Varian. The economics professor showed Google they could collect data from search engine users to accomplish three things.

First, was to pioneer behavioral advertising. By monitoring and aggregating the web-surfing and online transactions of its users Google could deliver ads targeted to the user's interest profile. Second, was to personalize data tracking that would enable Google to create a screen addictive experience. That's why we might see most everyone in a doctor's office waiting room glued to their smartphone or tablet computer screens until told "the doctor is ready to see you." Third, was to keep track of us everywhere, in a progressive number of ways. As computers become ever more powerful and compact, they have us under virtually constant surveillance. Our smartphones use cell tower coordinates to track our location as we move; embedded microphones learn from our conversations, whether those conversations be during phone calls or merely ambient to the presence of a seemingly idle smartphone; built-in cameras learn of our unspoken behavioral patterns, much to CNN contributor Jeffrey Toobin's everlasting shame.

Limiting Big Tech's oligopoly power will require a three-pronged attack.

First, is to enforce existing antitrust laws. The Justice Department must take the lead because the oligopoly members are so wealthy that few competitors are able to pay the legal fees required for a lengthy litigation, which Big Tech can stretch-out via a multitude of insincere motions. One of the remedies that might be immediately pursued is divestiture of YouTube by Google.

---

7 Josh Hawley, *The Tyranny of Big Tech*, 126-129,

Second, is to outlaw practices common among the online Big Tech platforms for which analogous practices in the terrestrial World are rare. One example is the way that Amazon copies products offered by third party vendors in its Amazon Marketplace online market. In October 2020 the House Antitrust Subcommittee released a report explaining how the online giant had released products almost identical to those offered by fledgling third party vendors at the online platform thereby poaching the customers away from the small fry.[8]

Third, is to remove Section 230 exemptions from lawsuits for libel and censorship for all companies engaged in behavioral advertising. This will pragmatically require those companies choosing to continue behavioral advertising to give users clear methods for opting out of data collection. As a result, consumers will better understand how much of their information has been routinely used under present Section 230 regulations and empower them to selectively turn it off.

The "good faith" provisions of Section 230 should be reinstated. It will make Big Tech vulnerable to antitrust lawsuits for capricious, or politically motivated, censorship. Compliance will transform the companies into politically neutral online communications platforms much like the public square of old. Noncompliance will transform them into online publishers like Internet versions of newspapers and magazines, which will make them vulnerable to damages for the bad conduct of their contributors. Under such circumstances, they will become vulnerable to a contributor's libelous conduct. They must choose between being a cyberspace version of a public square or an online publisher.

Such corrective actions should be adopted at once. They are necessary antidotes to the so-called Identity Politics dogmas that will transform our institutions into racial, and gender, quota-driven organizations dictated from the top down by elite Washington bureaucrats.

---

8 Grace Dean, "House antitrust report accuses Amazon of using third party seller data to copy popular products ...," *Business Insider,* (October 7, 2020): https://tinyurl. com/2p8rpmu3

CHAPTER SIX:

ANTIRACISM

FROM THE CRT PERSPECTIVE, the remedy for America's alleged systemic racism is not race neutrality, but "antiracism."

In *How to Be an Antiracist* author Ibram Kendi writes that when he was in high school, he did not realize that "to say that something is wrong about a racial group is to say that something is inferior about that group [and] to say something is inferior about a racial group is to say a racist idea." That syllogism led him to conclude that "the opposite of "racist" isn't 'not racist.' It is 'antiracist.' One either believes that racial problems are rooted in groups of people—as would a racist—or locates the roots of problems in power and policies, as an antiracist."

In Kendi's analysis the cause of racially disparate outcomes, whether they be economic, educational, number of convicts, number of unwed mothers, or some other metric, is entirely due to society. Any suggestion that the conduct of the racial groups is responsible is not merely wrong, it is racist. He argues that anyone claiming to be "not racist" is unknowingly, but truly, racist.

He further contends that "racist" is not an offensive slur, but merely a valid descriptor. That way he can label his opponents as racist and simultaneously claim they have no reason to be offended. Consequently, he plays the race card frequently because he knows that "racist" is interpreted as a slur that enables him to preemptively silence his critics no matter how erroneous, illogical, and biased his remarks are. As a result, his allegedly victimized group is empowered to monopolize any so-called conversation about race. They are exempted from having to listen to others who might disagree with their viewpoints.[1]

---

1 Ibram Kendi, *How to Be an Antiracist*, 9-10, 18-20

Since his framework contends that only policy changes can equalize disparate outcomes between racial groups, he proposes a new constitutional amendment to form a U.S. Department of Antiracism (DOA). It would be empowered to nullify, veto, or abolish any law pertinent to racial equity. If blacks are underrepresented in any profession, such as airline pilots, investment bankers, or physicians, the DOA could require that the professions have proportional representation within whatever time dictated. Wall Street, airlines, and medical schools must comply or face stiff penalties. Whenever the professions must be licensed, as with pilots, physicians and investment bankers, the statistics may be easily tracked.

While the policy adjustments implied by antiracism doctrine may seem as if they are taken from a dystopian science fiction movie, many are already happening because of the combined power of feminist and racial extremists. No less of a so-called misogyny victim than billionaire Sheryl Sandberg—Facebook's number two executive—said in a 2017 interview, "We need to start paying women well and we need public and corporate policy to get there... When there are equal numbers of each gender doing the same sorts of jobs at the same sort of level, then there will be no gender gap."

In truth, Sandberg may be the World's most overpaid woman. Among all female leaders she is one of the most prone to stand in the spotlight when her company succeeds but is normally off camera when CEO Zuckerberg stands alone to face its critics. Several years ago, California adopted a law requiring publicly owned companies to each have a specified number of female board members. Other states followed with similar laws. Starting in 2020 California adopted laws requiring similar quotas for racial and ethnic minorities and other states followed. Since such laws require discrimination against males and whites they are being challenged in court. Some challenges allege violation of the applicable state constitutions and others claim violation of the U. S. constitution.

Although he admits to having been irresponsible during high school, Kendi claims that black culture is unfairly stigmatized by such conduct. He writes, "I screwed up. I could have studied harder. But some of my white friends should have studied harder too, and their failures and irresponsibilities didn't somehow tarnish their race." He's wrong. Many Anglo-Saxon whites do indeed recognize that they collectively need to improve relative to minorities such as Asian Americans and Ashkenazi Jews. According to Bret Stephens of *The New York Times*, "Ashkenazi Jews have the highest average IQ of any ethnic group for which there are reliable data. During the twentieth century, they made up about 3% of the U.S. population but won 27% of the America's Nobel Prizes... They account for more than half of World chess champions."[2]

Largely because the pertinent statistics are carefully guarded, it is difficult for outsiders to know the precise racial and ethnic demographics at top schools but there's little doubt that Asian Americans and Jews are disproportionately represented. Even when combined they represent less than 10% of America's population but comprise an estimated 30% of Yale's students.[3]

Undeniably, both blacks and whites have something to learn from them. One key is the value the two cultures put on education and family. In contrast to other U.S. families, Asian American homes are more stable, have lower divorce rates, and have fewer female headed households. Only 6% of Asian Americans are separated or divorced compared to 13% for whites and 15% for blacks. Additionally, half of blacks never married, considerably more than the 28% of whites and 31% of Asians. In 2016 sixty-one percent of black children under age 18 lived with a single parent as compared to twenty-six percent for whites."[4]

In 2011 a Yale Asian American law professor authored *Battle Hymn of the Tiger Mother,* which revealed insights about Asian student achievement. A lot is due to a Tiger mom culture, rooted in a respect

---

2 Ibram Kendi, *How to Be an Antiracist,* 93; Jessica Guynn, "New California Law Requires Racial Diversity," *USA Today,* (September 30, 2020): https://tinyurl.com/bdd8kv2h; Brian Melley, "California Law Says Corporate Boards Need Women. Is it legal?," *Associated Press* (December 1, 2021): https://tinyurl.com/2p85decf; Robert Booth, "Sheryl Sandberg Calls for Policy Changes," *The Guardian,* (July 30, 2017): https://tinyurl.com/2p9yzeb7

3 Iman Ghosh, "Visualizing Population by Race," *Visual Capitalist,* (December 28, 2020): https://tinyurl.com/nyrj5tr7; Yale University, Hillel Guide: https://tinyurl.com/bddb84ma; College Factual, Yale University: Student Racial-Ethnic Demographics: https://tinyurl.com/2p996x5s

4 National Healthy Marriage Resource Center, "Asian & Pacific Islander,": https://tinyurl.com/yc6cb5h5; Black Demographics, "Households,": https://tinyurl.com/ms228h4f; Lewis Wirth, "Education for Survival: The Jews," *American Journal of Sociology,* V. 48, N. 6 (May, 1943), 682-91; Zenitha Prince, "Higher Percentage of Black Children Live With Single Mothers," *Afro News,* (December 31, 2016: https://tinyurl.com/2p833cam

for ancestors and an emphasis on accomplishment. Tiger parents inform their children that they are indebted to parents and ancestors for the sacrifices made earlier to enable the present generation to have an opportunity for a better life. Failing to take advantage of that opportunity is regarded as a nearly unforgiveable mistake.

Education is a cornerstone of Asian culture. Whereas Western parenting is generally permissive, Tiger parents feel a responsibility to prepare their children with marketable skills such as scientific and language proficiency. Together with a sound work ethic, such skills give children the confidence and discipline needed to compete successfully. Tiger parents also encourage children to excel in at least one non-academic field such as athletics or music.[5]

But Kendi need not look to non-black ethnic minorities such as Asian Americans and Jews as productive role models for African Americans. He can instead find inspiration among black groups that immigrated to America from the Caribbean or Africa. Instead, he resents them for supposedly having a condescending attitude toward African Americans. They do well, he argues, because all immigrant classes are more motivated than those of us who have lived in the United States for generations. While some immigrants may agree, many also tell tales of rejection and discrimination by multi-generation Americans. Among their oppressors are African Americans. Kendi admits that he and his public-school classmates ridiculed black refugee immigrants but ironically does not see himself as an oppressor.[6]

Kendi utterly rejects cultural differences as an explanation for the superior performance of Caribbean and African immigrants. When he concedes that black youths are more likely to commit crimes than white youths, he adds that there is little difference between the crime rate for white and black youths who are employed. Instead of investigating *why* whites are more likely employed, he attributes the higher black unemployment rate to racial discrimination. Since people are genetically 99.9% the same, he can see no other explanation. Therefore, the antiracist solution is to give more jobs to black youths, even if they haven't earned them by doing the job search required to get hired.

---

5 Grace Liu, "Why Tiger Moms are Great," *CNN*, (May 17, 2013): https://tinyurl. com/2p9hdbvr

6 Ibram Kendi, *How to Be an Antiracist*, 66-68

He is blind to the possibility that putting more blacks into jobs they did not earn implies that employers must tolerate a lower collective performance among their employees. Mandatory racial hiring quotas is merely a cost of doing business under Kendi's proposed dictatorial Department of Antiracism, but in a capitalistic society it spells bankruptcy for participating employers. Nowhere in *How to Be an Antiracist* does Kendi suggest that pro basketball and football teams should be racially blended in proportion to the race mixture for America at large. Nowhere does he suggest that the teams would be equally good even though the added white players are 99.9% genetically the same as the blacks that must hypothetically be cut from the teams for the sake of racial equity.[7]

Although Kendi claims to deplore racial stereotypes he disclosed his own typecast projection of Southern whites when he moved from metropolitan New York to a Virginia high school located in metropolitan Washington. His preformed imaginings about the neighboring whites traumatized him. Although 1999 Northern Virginia was not Southern in any traditional sense the then fifteen-year-old Kendi wrote, "Our first night there, I stayed up all night, occasionally looking out the window, worried that the Ku Klux Klan would arrive any minute... [A]s an urban black Northerner, I looked down on the cultures of non-urban blacks, especially Southerners, the very people I was surrounded by... I walked around during those early months at Stonewall Jackson [High] with an unspoken arrogance."

His arrogance did, however, lead to a discovery: "Whoever creates a cultural standard usually puts himself at the top of the hierarchy." The revelation was a milestone on his road toward discerning cultural relativity. He quotes anthropologist Ashley Montagu: "All cultures must be judged in relation to their own history, and all individuals and groups in relation to their cultural history, and not by the standard of any single culture." The white man's culture is not the only standard. Black culture, Kendi reasons, must not be compared to white culture in terms of superiority or inferiority. As an antiracist he sees "all cultures in all of their differences ... as equals." In essence he asserts that there is no good or bad culture. The black culture of the hood is not morally inferior to the white culture of the suburbs. They are merely different.

---

7 Ibram Kendi, *How to Be an Antiracist,* 52

Yet such logic implies that the Jihad Culture of radical Islam behind the 2001 attacks on the New York World Trade Center twin towers was only different from America's culture, not morally defective. Does he really believe that radical Jihad Culture is merely just different, and not morally wrong? Perhaps more to the point, is he suggesting that the antebellum South was merely a different culture that "should not [be judged] by the arbitrary standard of any single culture?" If so, he contradicts his own arguments for removing Confederate statues.

Truthfully, however, he undoubtedly realizes that cultures are likely to have both good and bad components. No doubt a tolerance for benign cultural differences enriches humanity. The ethnic restaurants of New York and other great cities are one example. Another was the advent of rock & roll that resulted from an overlap of African American and country music genres. Even the white Southerners of the postbellum era had a compensating grace. They dispensed with slavery by voting for the 1865 Thirteenth Amendment. If Kendi's concept of cultural relativism is not flexible enough to excuse slavery 150 years after it ended, it should not excuse the murder, rioting, arson, and looting by blacks during the summer of 2020 prompted by mostly phony charges of police brutality against blacks.

By stating that "Racial-group behavior is a figment of the racist's imagination" Kendi's argument gets tied in knots trying to make a distinction between culture and group behavior. While conceding that driving around in a convertible with rap music played at the volume of rhythmic nuclear explosions might be a significant cultural characteristic, he argues that the practice is not a black behavioral trait determined genetically. That point is phony because few critics believe that such obnoxious behavior is genetically determined just as few blacks believe that a penchant for cowboy boots and chewing tobacco is genetically embedded among all whites. Nevertheless, he insists upon labeling any criticism of black culture as racist.

In 2016 black columnist Jason Riley of the *Wall Street Journal* wrote: "Although black civil rights leaders like to point to a supposedly racist criminal justice system to explain why our prisons house so many black men, it's been obvious for decades that the real culprit is black behavior." Kendi focused on the last two words, "black behavior."

He took them as proof that Riley was adducing criminal behavior to be endemic to black men, whereas the newspaperman was merely connecting obvious black cultural practices with high crime rates.

Kendi similarly criticized W. E. B. DuBois, a radical black civil rights leader of the early twentieth century, in the same manner because in 1897 DuBois opined, "[T]he first and greatest step toward the settlement of the present friction between the races ... lies in the correction of immorality, crime, and laziness among the Negros themselves, which remains a heritage of slavery." Kendi cannot see that DuBois used "heritage of slavery" in the same context that Kendi uses "black culture." The faults were not inborn traits of all blacks but merely a legacy of slave dependency. In short, his attempt to draw a distinction between "group behavior" and "culture" is an obfuscation to exempt blacks collectively from responsibility for subpar results. Fortunately for Kendi, his parents rejected such arguments when they raised him to adulthood.[8]

While Kendi focuses upon an alleged privilege gap between blacks and whites, he is largely unaware of his own privileges. He is the child of a prosperous two-parent family. Both parents took an active interest in his education. Yet he seems to think he would have been more privileged to have been born into a single parent white family in Appalachia.

Although he attended a predominantly black public high school, he was in the International Baccalaureate group, a program for gifted students. When the school announced a competition for speeches honoring Dr. Martin Luther King, another student convinced Kendi to enter. He overslept on the morning of his speech. Although not arriving until the competition was over, he was given a second chance after the student that motivated him to participate begged the judges to reconvene and let him speak. He won the contest but fails to consider whether one of the white students at Stonewall Jackson High would have been permitted to present their speech if they had overslept.

During his senior year as a college undergraduate, he decided to go to graduate school. His parents forked over $1,000 for a preparatory course to boost his Graduate Record Exam test results by an advertised 200 points. He concluded the course was racist because most of the

---

8 Ibram Kendi, *How to Be an Antiracist*, 90-91, 94, 96, 132

students were white. Based upon the price, it's more likely that any discrimination by the course administrators was linked to economic class, rather than race.[9]

He also believes that part of the reason blacks score lower in standardized testing is due to cultural relativism. He argues that the tests were originally designed for white people who have different cultural and learning traits. "Standardized tests have become," says Kendi, "the most effective racist weapon ever devised to objectively degrade Black and Brown minds and legally exclude their bodies from prestigious schools."

During a 1968 strike when 54,000 teachers walked off the job, New York's African American Teachers Association (AATA) offered similar excuses years before Kendi was born. The union rejected behavior norms they considered to be Western. Among them were individualism, conformity, hard work, discipline, merit, competition, and materialism. They condemned any form of cognitive testing. They criticized the teaching of capitalism and Western culture. They wanted more black studies. In contrast they regarded Western culture as a form of white supremacy and imperialism, which should be minimized if not blocked entirely. Even though 1960s black militants disavowed materialism, it was obvious that both the black and white communities were equally selfish. In *Reckoning with Race* Gene Dattel adds:

In the AATA's view, the white man was to be blamed for the black condition, hence Western culture must be removed from the classroom. Highly structured educational methods, combined with respect for authority—the techniques of white Western middle-class teachers—would stifle black creativity and lead black students to "misbehave and squirm." [According to one black principal], "Black children are innovators, inventors, creators, actors, and performers. They like exciting styles, fashions, colors, and constant change... [These] healthy bubbling energies were evidence of rare distributive talents which many whites lack" and didn't understand.

---

9 Ibram Kendi, *How to Be an Antiracist*, 100, 104-06

In contrast to Western style education, blacks advocated a program based on distinct black values. They profess a vague attachment to cooperation, community, and ethnic-group consciousness, with seemingly no interest in mastering reading, writing, and mathematical skills. A "unique black culture" precluded the competition inherent in a merit system and fostered a separatist, even belligerent, attituded toward whites. The word "authentic" became a workhorse description for this racially separate identity—an orientation that subordinated the individual to his or her black group affiliation. Those who did not abide the racial peer pressure were branded as "traitors or Uncle Toms." There would be no compromise with white Western norms.

The above arguments, and the attempts to implement them, were unsuccessful. Since they have not worked for over fifty years it is time to drop them. Even Kendi could never have won a National Book Award unless he had learned reading, writing, and mathematics. Moreover, ethnic division demoralizes America, making us a weaker country. Kendi is so obsessed with imagining systemic racism and identifying those allegedly atop the racial hierarchy, he fails to realize that ethnic division is indistinguishable from ethnic hierarchy. Promoting such division is sheer folly for a society that seeks to achieve genuine equality.[10]

Although criticisms of traditional teaching are once again all the rage, the evidence between 1968 and the present is that racial and ethnic minorities should not point to racial discrimination as an excuse for bad academic performance. Consider the case of Garfield High school in east Los Angeles, an area populated by ethnic minorities of low academic achievement.

In 1974 the school hired a Bolivian immigrant, Jamie Escalante to teach math. When he learned that the school might lose its accreditation, he offered to challenge students by teaching them calculus. His goal was to get them to pass the Advance Placement calculus exam. Although unable to assemble his first class of volunteers

---

10 Gene Dattel, *Reckoning with* Race, 178-79; John Rosales and Tim Walker, "The Racist Beginnings of Standardized Testing," *neaNow,* (March 20, 2012): https://tinyurl.com/yc3e8fe2

until 1978, he persuaded five students to join. He encouraged them by explaining that knowledge of calculus would help them get into good colleges and find good jobs. Initially the school administration opposed him but within a few years he started getting support from a new principal.

Escalante inspired his students. They developed self-respect because the work was hard, yet they discovered they could do it. At the end of the 1978-79 school year, two of the five students passed the AP calculus exam. The following year, the class size increased to nine students, seven of whom passed the AP calculus test. By 1981, the class had increased to 15 students, 14 of whom passed.

His classes first gained media attention in 1982 when 18 of students passed the AP exam. From a statistical viewpoint, the results were so unexpected that the Educational Testing Service suspected the students had cheated. Fourteen were asked to re-take the exam. Twelve agreed and did well enough to have their original scores re-instated.

In 1983 thirty-three students took the exam and thirty passed. In 1987 his students were taking either the AB version of the test or the BC version. That year 83 students passed the AB version and 12 passed the BC version. When education experts asked that he share his secret, he answered, "The key ... is a very simple and time-honored tradition: hard work for teacher and student alike." President Ronald Reagan was among his class visitors.

Although he stayed at Garfield until the early 1990s, his classes became so popular their attendance exceeded the maximums allowed by the teachers' union. In 1991 the number of Garfield students taking Advanced Placement exams in math and other subjects totaled 570. At the height of Escalante's success Garfield students were entering Southern California University in such great numbers that they outnumbered those admitted from the working-class neighborhoods of all other east Los Angeles high schools. Since his success embarrassed the union, he left for a teaching post in Sacramento. Thereafter he also became a strong proponent for English-only class instruction.[11]

---

11 Wikipedia, "Jamie Escalante: https://en.wikipedia.org/wiki/Jaime_Escalante

Although Kendi's narrative of America's historical racism toward blacks is well footnoted, he's sometimes unfairly selective in his citations, leaving an impression of tailoring evidence to support a predetermined conclusion. More significantly, he sees antiblack racism everywhere in the past. One example is a paragraph citing historical white violence toward blacks in which he states, "Seceding Texas legislators in 1861 complained of not receiving more federal 'appropriations for protection ... against ruthless savages.'" Either he fails to explain, or does not realize, that the statement applied to Indians, not blacks. Comanche warriors killed both blacks and whites. They were not subdued until 1875, fourteen years after Texas seceded.[12]

In a second example involving the 2012 Trayvon Martin shooting by George Zimmerman near Orlando Kendi misrepresents Zimmerman as racist and exaggerated his criminal record. Zimmerman was a registered Democrat and had voted for Barack Obama. Despite media pressure and NBC's deceptive editing of 911 tapes, FBI investigators concluded there was no evidence that Zimmerman was racist.

Eight years earlier Zimmerman started an insurance agency with a black partner. One year before the shooting, Zimmerman attended a municipal hearing where he publicly criticized the police for abusing blacks, particularly an attack he witnessed on a homeless man. When he was twenty-two Zimmerman was arrested for shoving an undercover policeman dressed in civilian clothes who was trying to overpower a Zimmerman friend at a bar. That was his only conviction.[13]

When he attended college at historically black Florida A&M, Kendi became enraged when George W. Bush won the presidency over Al Gore. He was convinced Gore would have won except for Florida's supposed voter suppression rules. Although Bush won the state by only 247 votes, and Kendi later learned that thousands of Florida A&M students were registered voters that chose not to vote, he prefers to

---

12 Ibram Kendi, *How to Be an Antiracist*, 70

13 Ibram Kendi, *How to Be an Antiracist*, 223-35; "Zimmerman Alleged Police Brutality," *Associated Press*, (May 24, 2012): https://tinyurl.com/dsw6cd77; Michael Dougherty, "NBC: We're Sorry We Edited the Trayvon Martin Tape ...," *NBC* (April 4, 2012): https://tinyurl.com/2p82z2ts; Wikipedia, "George Michael Zimmerman," https://en.wikipedia.org/wiki/George_Zimmerman

blame so-called systemic racism for Gore's loss even though his A&M classmates could have put Gore in the White House if they had merely cast their votes.[14]

Finally, Kendi may wish to examine the life expectancy gap between whites and blacks. At birth white males have a 76-year life expectancy compared to 72 years for black males. Kendi's autobiography may provide one explanation. During the last four months of 2017 when focused on combating "white nationalists who were running and terrorizing the United States," Kendi ignored weight loss and bloody diarrhea. By Thanksgiving he was bedridden and throwing up. By Christmas things became acute. A January 10, 2018, colonoscopy revealed Stage 4 colon cancer. It had advanced so far that the statistical recovery probability was only 12%. Even though he became one of the fortunate few, his survival probabilities could have been improved if he had been self-reliant enough to consult a doctor earlier.

Nonetheless, Kendi writes, "To be antiracist is to let me be me, by myself, by my imperfect self." Nearly everyone can applaud a leader who asks Americans to let him, and his followers, be themselves—even their imperfect selves—so long as they extend the same courtesy to their opponents. But Kendi and his acolytes don't reciprocate the courtesy. They leverage cancel culture to silence dissenters by falsely labeling them racists.[15]

---

14 Ibram Kendi, *How to Be an Antiracist*, 124-25

15 Ibram Kendi, *How to Be an Antiracist*, 205, 232-37

CHAPTER SEVEN:

REWRITING REALITY

A BIG PART OF CRITICAL RACE THEORY and Identity Politics is a sinister reframing of the history of Western civilization and America. The bias is so marked that it goes beyond a mere revision and becomes an attempted rewriting of reality. The result is an imaginary reality contained within a goldfish bowl where all CRT and Identity Victimhood followers swim. Any fact not found in the goldfish bowl is deemed to be unreal. Two of the biggest influences on such rewritings are Howard Zinn's *A Peoples History of the United States* and the "1619 Project" from the *New York Times*.

When published in 1980, Zinn said his book purposely scrutinized a different side of history from the traditional "fundamental nationalist glorification of our country." His story is largely one of exploitation and manipulation of the masses by rigged systems of government for the benefit of the wealthy and other elites. It adopts the familiar Marxist and CRT agenda of defining history as a conflict between oppressed and oppressors. It was a 1980 runner-up for the National Book Award. Although traditional historians have since criticized the book for blatant omissions, uncritical reliance on dubious sources, and a failure to account for opposing interpretations of historical facts, it has sold over two million copies. Many high schools and colleges assign the book for classes.

When a *Young People's* version was released in 2007, Professor Zinn explained his book in a letter to the *New York Times*: "My history...describes the inspiring struggle of those who have fought slavery and racism, of labor organizers who led strikes for the rights of working people, of the socialists and others who protested war and militarism. My hero is not Theodore Roosevelt, who loved war and congratulated a general after the massacre of Filipino villagers at the turn of the century, but Mark Twain who denounced the massacre and satirized imperialism. I want young people to understand that ours is a beautiful country, but it has been taken over by men who have no respect for human rights or constitutional liberties. Our people are basically decent and caring, and our highest ideals are expressed in the Declaration of Independence, which says that all of us have an equal right to "life liberty and the pursuit of happiness." The history of our country...is a striving, against corporate robber barons and war makers, to make those ideals a reality—and all of us, of whatever age, can find immense satisfaction in becoming part of that.[1]

Like CRT, Zinn's history is not merely the telling of a story but the initiation of a social justice movement. Traditional histories built around the great men of the past, he says, "add up to exactly the simplistic history fed to young people over the generations, which my book tries to replace." He adds, customary "history produces a submissive population, always looking for saviors on high. I prefer that...[students] learn that we cannot depend on established authority to keep us out of war and to create economic justice, but rather that solving these problems depends on us, the citizenry, and on the great social movements we have created." Zinn's aim was never to equip his readers to understand the past. His goal was to persuade them to reject the present and dedicate themselves to his vision for the American future. In short, he wanted students to hate America so that it could be torn down and rebuilt to conform to his vision.[2]

Zinn's teachings are a branch of Critical Theory. In his analysis, however, the conflicting victims and oppressors may be identified with multiple delineations such as race, gender, and economic class. Governments, he argues, are not neutral. If not proactively regulated, they will represent the interests of the dominant classes. It is hard to imagine a better preamble to the present doctrines of Critical Race Theory, antiracism, and Identity Victimhood.

Zinn's menacing narrative causes his followers to dishonor many previously valued historical figures by destroying their statues and changing the names of schools and streets that memorialize them.

---

1 Howard Zinn, "Making History," *New York Times: Letter to Editor,* (July 1, 2007): https://tinyurl.com/2p9638wt

2 *Ibid.*

They attempt to silence objections to such measures via the usual cancel culture methods that can be triggered by mere accusations of racism or misogyny.

One example is Andrew Jackson, which President Biden wants to disgrace by removing his image from the $20 bill. Zinn wrote of Jackson: "If you look through high school and elementary school textbooks in American history, you will find Jackson the frontiersman, soldier, democrat, man of the people—not Jackson the slaveholder, land speculator, executioner of dissident soldiers, exterminator of Indians." He doesn't mention that Jackson was the first commoner elected President after a string of six aristocrats. Nor does he mention that Jackson peacefully stopped South Carolina from seceding in 1832, even though the Southern President was sympathetic to some of the state's complaints. He also fails to mention that Jackson was the only President to pay off the national debt. Jackson basically won the "Second" American War for Independence after his victory at the Battle of New Orleans convinced Europe that America could not be easily conquered.[3]

The deceased Zinn's work continues today at the Zinn Education Project website, which is promoted to public school teachers across the country. In true Zinn fashion, one editorial contributor wrote a review of a children's book describing slavery at George Washington's Mount Vernon home as follows:

Although a worthwhile effort...the title [*George's People*] implies a certain legitimacy to Washington's "ownership" of people. Legally, morally, and politically, people who were enslaved by Washington were property without any rights... They were his property.

Many of the book's pictures are of slave reenactors...Most are smiling or have neutral faces. You would be hard-pressed to find an unhappy person. The book focuses on the individual lives of those enslaved ... [including one] young woman, beaten by the farm manager...with

---

3 Howard Zinn, *A People's History of the United States*, (New York: HarperCollins, 1999), 98, 130; Philip Leigh, "Six Reasons to Leave Andrew Jackson on the $20 bill," *The Hill*, (September 26, 2019); https://tinyurl.com/2p8h6hp8

Washington's approval... Missing from the book...is the brutality and dehumanization of slavery. Although Delano [the author] points repeatedly that slavery was bad, she fails to convey the all-sided harshness [of it.]

The most disturbing element of the book is that it tends to treat slavery as an issue of personal choice. The real heroes of the period were the abolitionists who called and fought for the immediate end of slavery, and the enslaved who resisted in myriad ways.[4]

The critic fails to remind young readers that there would be no America without George Washington. Nor does she mention that he risked his life to gain our freedom. That risk was not merely as a battlefield soldier. He was a revolutionary leader who might well have been executed if the revolution had failed. Finally, she does not mention that Washington voluntarily stepped down after two terms as President, virtually assuring that America would not devolve into a phony democratic Republic, such as Russia is presently, or a dictatorship, like France became after Napoleon declared himself Emperor in 1804.

Although Zinn's book is presently over forty years old, the "1619 Project" was released in 2019. Originally a collection of articles for a special edition of the *New York Times Magazine* its purpose was to "reframe our country's history." Project leader Nikole Hannah-Jones introduced the compilation by writing: "Our democracy's founding ideals were false when they were written. Conveniently left out of our founding mythology is the fact that one of the primary reasons some of the colonists decided to declare their independence from Britain was because they wanted to protect the institution of slavery." That opinion has been debunked by prominent historians such as Gordon Wood, James McPherson, and T. J. Stiles.

Despite errors disclosed by renowned historians and multiple corrections by the *New York Times*, the Project won Hannah-Jones a Pulitzer Prize in 2020 and opened the door for a teaching post at Howard University. The Project is merely a rendition of CRT's bogus

---

4 Clarence Lusane, "Whitewashing Our First President," *Zinn Education Project*: https://tinyurl.com/2p99p2cm

interpretation of American history. One of the original articles titled, "American Capitalism is Brutal. You Can Trace That Back to the Plantation," underscores the link to nineteenth century Marxism and from it through the Frankfurt School to modern Critical Race Theory. Despite its falsehoods, the Project is taught in Washington, D. C., Buffalo, Newark, and Chicago. Buffalo's public schools have used it in grades 7 through 12 since February 2020. Chicago's public schools are teaching the "1619 Project" using curriculum guides from the Pulitzer Center.[5]

The destruction and removal of Confederate statues, especially during the past few years, symbolizes the downfall of our culture from within. It reflects the "Fifth Column" formula the Frankfurt School Marxists developed in the 1920s and 30s. They realized that culture is the glue unifying a country. In America, it is the tradition created out of the chaos of our revolution. Whenever the structure of a culture is disrupted, chaos unwittingly returns. Eventually traditionalists will do anything to defend themselves against that return because chaos translates to a society in ruin. Time and again, the result has been countries like Cuba and the Soviet Union.

Elite politicians, media personalities, and educators, argue that opposition to CRT is resistance to teaching students about America's historical flaws. That's a lie. There's a difference between teaching *about* CRT and teaching CRT. The former informs about a theory whereas the latter uncritically promotes a *doctrine* that necessitates the adoption of intentionally discriminatory antiracist remedies. There can be no hope of preserving Confederate memory, or even respect for men like Robert E. Lee, if Critical Race Theory and Identity Victimhood continue to grow.

The great irony about those wanting to vandalize, destroy, and remove Confederate statues is that their objective is directly opposite to that of Abraham Lincoln's during the Civil War 160 years ago. Lincoln sought to reunite the country whereas those who deface Confederate memorials are dividing it. Nowhere is the point more obvious than in the memory of General Robert E. Lee. Today's historians focus on reinterpreting obscure incidents, or alleged incidents, to reframe him

---

5 Senator Ted Cruz, "Critical Race Theory," *Leadership Institute,* (November 2021): https://tinyurl.com/f3tcyx2w

as first and foremost a racist obsessed with hatred for blacks. Not only are the interpretations deliberately sinister and sometimes patent lies, but they miss a greater truth about Lee. While today's social justice warriors are doing all they can to break America apart, they fail to see how Lee's leadership—call it myth if you insist—was a powerful force that helped reunite the country.

During his postbellum years from 1865 to his death in 1870 his absence of resentment, common among the defeated of any age, raised him high above sectional hatreds to become a role model of reconciliation. Although he wished Southerners to remain faithful to their traditions of honor, virtue, courage, and hospitality, he wanted them to drop any feelings that would impede reconciliation. He saw only ruin in continued bitterness.

As he was traveling through one Southern town years after the war, a mother widowed by the war stepped forward to introduce her two young sons while loudly expressing her hatred of Yankees. No doubt she assumed that his feelings were like hers. Although he stopped momentarily to greet the family, before moving on he said, "Madam, don't bring up your sons to detest the United States Government. Recollect that we form but one country, now. Abandon all these local animosities and make your sons Americans." What better inscription for a Lee statue than that?[6]

Although it is true that Lee was sometimes a slaveholder, it was not often. At age 22 he graduated second in his West Point class the very month his mother died in 1829 leaving perhaps a dozen slaves to her sons. Robert, however, had little use for slaves during the military career he was just then starting. More as a gesture of responsibility toward a dependent than an act of entitled ownership, he took an aged houseslave with him on his first assignment to Savannah where he thought the older man might benefit from Georgia's milder climate. Between then and when he turned fifty years-old in 1857, he had little to do with slaves. In 1857 his father-in-law died and left Lee's wife nearly two hundred slaves. Most were at the Arlington family estate across the Potomac River from Washington City.

---

6 Gamaliel Bradford, *Lee the American,* (Cambridge: The Riverside Press, 1912), 98

Although the slaves belonged to his wife, Lee was the estate executor. The deceased's will stipulated that the slaves be set free within five years of his death but also required the executor to set aside monetary legacies for each of the deceased's granddaughters. The unprofitable condition of the plantation required Lee to work the slaves to fund the legacies. Nonetheless, he set all the slaves free a month after his December 1862 Civil War victory at the Battle of Fredericksburg, which was two months tardy. By then, however, many had runaway since Arlington had been occupied by federal forces for the previous eighteen months. In contrast, the slaves in Union General Ulysses Grant's wife's family were not freed until January 1865, three years after those of General Lee's wife.[7]

While Lee was admittedly a slaveholder on occasion, he was also a man of his time and place. He was born into a place and era when slaveholding was common. Everybody is influenced by the time and place of their birth and childhood years, whether they admit it or not. Some politicians deeply honored today may one day be criticized for holding beliefs that are later discredited. Consider, for example, how President Obama might be dishonored if future Americans condemn abortions. No doubt his advocates will plead that he should be respected for qualities other than his endorsement of infanticide.

A similar rationale can be made for Robert E. Lee. His perspectives on slavery and blacks were consistent with those of most contemporary Americans. In 1854, for example, Abraham Lincoln publicly stated that he opposed slavery in the western territories because he wanted such lands reserved for "free white people." In his 1858 debates with Stephen Douglas for an Illinois Senate seat he remarked, "I am not, nor ever have been, in favor of bringing about in any way the social and political equality of the white and black races. I am not nor ever have been in favor of making voters or jurors of negroes, nor of qualifying them to hold office, nor to intermarry with white people; and I will say in addition to this that there is a physical difference between the white and black races which I believe will forever forbid the two races living together on terms of social and political equality. And inasmuch as they

---

7 Emory Thomas, *Robert E. Lee: A Biography* (New York: W. W. Norton, 1995), 57-58; Clifford Dowdey, *Lee,* (New York: Skyhorse Publishing, 2015), 112-13, 331

cannot so live, while they do remain together there must be the position of superior and inferior, and I as much as any other man am in favor of having the superior position assigned to the white race."[8]

Like Lincoln, there is much to admire about Robert E. Lee despite the racial attitudes he shared with most Americans, including Northerners. He was, for example, the general most admired by his troops on either side of the Civil War. After nine months of temporary duty in Georgia and Tennessee, for example, Lee's third (of three) corps joyfully rejoined his Virginia army a week before its first battle against Grant. When the soldiers caught sight of Lee during a welcoming review, one wrote: "[A] wave of sentiment swept over the field. Each man seemed to feel the bond which held us all to Lee. The effect was that of a military sacrament, in which we pledged anew our lives." Another observer recorded the same event: "As Lee rode up to the [flags], and the men caught sight of his well-known figure, a wild and prolonged cheer fraught with a feeling that filled all hearts, ran along the lines and rose to the heavens. Hats were thrown high, and many persons became almost frantic with emotion."[9]

Since Lee's army had regiments from every Confederate state his troops' affection, and respect, for him also became nearly universal among civilian Southerners. Less than a month after Lee's surrender Union Lieutenant General Ulysses Grant wrote of Lee's unprecedented reputation on May 5, 1865, "All of the [Southern] people except a few political leaders in the South will accept whatever he does as right and will be guided to a great extent by his example." As Shelby Foote put it, "Lee's veterans fought less for a cause than they did for a tradition. Mainly, though, Lee's veterans fought for Lee, or at any rate the pride they felt as they watched him ride among them."[10]

They also demonstrated their admiration for the general during combat. It was most famously demonstrated at the Battle of the Wilderness when the armies of Lee and Grant first met in battle. On the morning of May 6, 1864, the Confederates were in a desperate

---

8 David Herbert Donald, *Lincoln,* (Jonathan Cape, London, 1995), 221

9 Gary Gallagher, *Lee and His Generals in War and Memory,* (Baton Rouge: Louisiana State University Press, 1998), 3

10 Robert Phillips, *Shelby Foote: Novelist and Historian,* (Jackson: University of Mississippi Press, 1992), 201; Clifford Dowdey, *Lee,* 641

situation as their defense line was collapsing from a federal attack. Lee felt the situation was hopeless until a reinforcing brigade of Texas and Arkansas troops arrived in the nick of time.

As the brigade deployed for a successful counterattack Lee joined them. He appeared intent on leading the charge on his horse Traveller. A group of nearby soldiers noticed the general's foolhardy plan and started a shout that travelled down the line, "Lee to the rear!" Some men pleaded with him directly, saying, "Go back, General Lee, go back." A sergeant took hold of the Traveller's reins to stop the horse. Prompted by such urgings, Lee turned back and rode off through cheering Confederate troops. "I thought him at that moment the grandest specimen of manhood I ever beheld," one witness later recounted.

Lee earned the soldiers' respect by way of his exemplary conduct in at least three ways. First, he shared their hardships. After winning the Battle of Fredericksburg fifty miles north of Richmond in early December 1862 he journeyed back to the capital city to confer with President Jefferson Davis. He could have stayed warm in Richmond through the Christmas season, but he instead returned to be among his troops in their crude winter quarters along the Rappahannock River. While most army commanders would appropriate the home of a nearby resident for use as a headquarters (HQ) post, Lee normally slept in a tent or a crude dugout in winter. By contrast, Union General Ulysses Grant put his HQ at the Widow Crisp's house while his men slept under the February snow at Tennessee's Battle of Fort Donelson. Similarly, when his army was attacked by surprise two months later at Pittsburg Landing on the Tennessee River, Grant was sleeping ten miles upstream at the Cherry Mansion.[11]

The second way Lee earned his soldiers' admiration was by taking responsibility for his failures rather than blaming others. Perhaps the best example was when Lee took full accountability for his army's first decisive defeat at the Battle of Gettysburg on July 3, 1863. At the end of the month Lee wrote President Davis, "No blame can be attached to the army for its failure to accomplish what was projected by me... I alone am to blame." A week later he offered to resign, but Davis turned him down.

---

11 Clifford Dowdey, *Lee's Last Campaign,* (New York: Skyhorse Publishing, 1999), 34, 153-54

After his anxious gamble to win on the third day at Gettysburg when Pickett's Charge failed, one of Lieutenant General James Longstreet's staff officers saw Lee meeting the returning survivors: "It is all my fault," he said, "I take it all. Get together now men, we shall yet beat them." The staff officer later wrote, "I saw no man fail him." A British observer also saw Lee meet the survivors: "All this will come out right in the end," he said. "We'll talk it over afterward, but in the meantime all good men must rally." (He was anticipating a federal counterattack.) An officer in the First Virginia regiment heard Lee tell Pickett, "General, your men have done all that men can do. The fault is entirely my own." As returning officers arrived, he repeated over and over: "It is all my fault." Such conduct is rare but an infinitely valuable leadership example. Contrast it with the evasions of President Biden, Defense Secretary Lloyd Austin, and Joint Chiefs of Staff Chairman General Mark Milley about the 2021 Afghanistan debacle.[12]

Lee also earned admiration as perhaps the best example of an army commander who consistently held the respect of both his soldiers and superiors. When Davis replied to Lee's resignation offer after Gettysburg the President wrote, "To ask me to substitute you for someone in my judgement more fit to command is to demand an impossibility." No other leader of a field army on either side persistently held such a symbiotic relationship with his superiors. Yet Lee was dutiful to Davis without being submissive.[13]

Ultimately Lee was admired most for a persistent spirit of self-denial, the source of his leadership qualities. Whether he was inspired by the "let [the follower] deny himself" directions in the gospels of Mathew and Luke, is speculative. But on one visit to Northern Virginia after the war a young mother brought her baby to him to be blessed. He took the infant in his arms, looked at it and then at her and said, "Teach him he must deny himself." That is all.

Oscar Wilde once observed that "Life imitates Art far more than Art imitates Life." Indeed, critics of the Confederacy often cite the chivalric novels of Sir Walter Scott (1771-1832) for shaping the Southern

---

12 Glenn Tucker, *High Tide at Gettysburg,* (Gettysburg: Stan Clark Military Books, 1995), 376-77, 432; Lt. Col. Arthur J. L. Fremantle, *Three Months in the Southern States,* (Lincoln: University of Nebraska Press, 1991), 267-69

13 David J. Eicher, *The Longest Night,* (New York: Simon & Schuster, 2001), 553

aristocrat's self-image. Southerners related to Scott's novels of gallant little Scotland fighting as the underdog to retain her cultural identity against the pressures of her more powerful English neighbors. Scott's *Ivanhoe* (1819) was so popular in the region that some Southern towns organized medieval jousting tournaments where antebellum grandees could act out their fantasies of knighthood, honor, courage, loyalty, nobility, courtesy, and chivalry. Such dreams would become deadly real during the War Between the States. Even presently some historians refer to Lee in such Arthurian terms—critics in ridicule, and devotees in admiration. When he was President of Washington College after the war, one freshman student who was eager to perform well asked for a copy of the college rules. Lee replied, "We have but one rule here and it is that every student must be a gentleman."[14]

Similarly, white Southern authors were among the most effective agents for racial reconciliation during the twentieth century. A black physician is the most noble character in Carson McCullers 1940 novel, *The Heart is a Lonely Hunter*. William Faulkner's 1948 *Intruder in the Dust* revolves around a black farmer falsely accused of murdering a white man. He is acquitted through the efforts of black and white teenagers and a spinster from an old Southern family. In 1949 Joe David Brown released *Stars in My Crown*, a novel for young readers in which the white protagonist shames a white mob into abandoning their attempt to lynch a black man. Brown's 1956 *Kings Go Forth* reveals a tragic injustice for a black woman who fell in love with a white Mississippian. She is avenged by a different white man who had also fallen in love with her. Harper Lee's 1960 *To Kill a Mockingbird* concerns a false rape accusation against a black in Depression Era Alabama. Each novel was sufficiently popular to be adapted into a feature length movie. Ultimately Southern life imitated the edifications of their stories.

When peppering him with implications of defending slavery for his failure to condemn Confederate statues in 2017, President Trump responded to reporters, "George Washington was a slaveholder...are we going to take down statues of Washington? How about Thomas Jefferson? What do you think about Thomas Jefferson?...Are we going to take down [his] statue? Because he was a major slaveowner."

---

14 Douglas Southall Freeman, *R. E. Lee: Volume 4*, (New York: Charles Scribner & Sons, 1948), 278

Although Trump's implication that statue vandalism might spread beyond Confederate figures has proven to be true, he was initially ridiculed for it. Some of the most acid mockers were academics. One example is Douglas Blackman of the University of Virginia's Miller Center. When he gave an interview to the *Washington Post* about Trump's remarks: "It's the difference between a monument to the founder of our nation [Washington] and a monument to a key figure [Lee] in an effort to break apart the nation. The kindest explanation of that [Trump's prediction] can only be ignorance and I don't say that to insult the President."[15]

Unfortunately, President Trump was correct. Confederate statues were just a starting point for the political Left. Their real objective is to demolish traditional America and attack the memory of the men who founded the country. Near the top of the list is the author of the Declaration of Independence, Thomas Jefferson. If they can persuade us to despise Jefferson and some of the other founders, they'll be on their way to transforming America into a country that hates our traditional values. America was not founded because her people were of a common race, as was typical elsewhere. The nation was founded on ideals that united us. America was organized as a constitutional republic with no ruling family, thereby proclaiming the political equality of all her citizens whom she invested with the freedom to pursue their own interests with minimal government interference.

Present attacks on the founders focus on what they did not do as opposed to what they did accomplish. Although they didn't abolish slavery, they did indeed organize the freest country in history. When founded, America had but three million people, the current population Iowa. At the time the thirteen colonies were little more than a remote backwater on the World stage, but they bloomed into one of the most powerful nations on Earth within a century and a quarter. The contrast between Jefferson's denunciations of slavery and his failure to put them into practice, make him an easy target. Yet the first gift Jefferson gave to America was her independence. His language of the "self-evident" truths left a lasting mark. His Declaration of Independence asserted that certain rights linked to those truths should be universal,

15 Jerrett Stepman, *The War on History*, (Washington, D. C.: Regnery Publishing, 2019), 69-70

not merely applicable to thirteen colonies. If Jefferson falls victim to cancel culture, there may be no stopping a George Washington takedown as well.

Although his participation in slavery is the obvious flaw in the reputation of a founder who wrote "all men are created equal," many Americans today believe that slavery was unique to our Southern states. In truth, slavery was legal in all thirteen colonies in 1776. In 1890 Lincoln's two private secretaries wrote in a ten-volume biography of the former President that, "[Lincoln] believed the people of the North were as responsible for slavery as the people of the South." Less than three months before the Civil War ended Lincoln told Secretary of State Seward, "If it was wrong in the South to hold slaves, it was wrong in the North to carry on the slave trade and sell them to the South." Moreover, during the four hundred years of trans-Atlantic slave trade only about four percent arrived in America. Most all the others went to Brazil and the Caribbean.[16]

Even though the Declaration's "all men are created equal" phrase was an obvious contradiction from the beginning, Martin Luther King took the correct perspective on it. He realized that slavery could not have been abruptly ended in 1776 without aborting the birth of our country. Thus, he interpreted Jefferson's Declaration as a "promissory note" to be redeemed at the right time. The Declaration ultimately made it impossible for slavery to continue indefinitely. When the Thirteenth Amendment ending slavery was ratified in December 1865 the pre-Carpetbagger, all-white legislatures of eight of the eleven former Confederate states voted in favor of it. A ninth, Florida, followed by the end of the same month.

According to Princeton Law Professor Robert George, nearly all his students declare that they would have been abolitionists had they lived in the South in the late 1850s. But he shows that only the tiniest fraction of them would have spoken out against slavery or lifted a finger to free the slaves. Most of them—and us—would have gone along. Many would have supported the slave system and happily benefitted from it.

---

16 David Donald, *Lincoln,* 560; John Nicolay and John Hay, *Abraham Lincoln: A History, Volume 10,* (New York: Century Publishers, 1890), 124

George tells the students that he will credit their abolitionist claims if they can show that in leading their present lives they have stood up for the rights of *unpopular* victims of injustice and where they have done so knowing all the following consequences:

1. They would be loathed and ridiculed by powerful individuals and institutions.

2. They would be abandoned by many of their friends.

3. They would be shouted down with vile names.

4. They would be denied valuable professional opportunities because of their moral witnessing.

5. They might even lose their jobs after such witnessing.

In short, he challenged the students to show where they have—at risk to themselves and their futures—stood up for a cause that is unpopular within the elite sectors of modern society.

Another professor, at the Oshkosh campus of Wisconsin University, revealed more distorted knowledge about slavery and Thomas Jefferson in a quiz he gave to 32 students. He discovered that 29 knew Jefferson was a slaveholder but only 3 knew that he had been President. Conversely, six students falsely believed that Benjamin Franklin had been President.

Historian Jerrett Stepman writes, "It is easy to condemn Jefferson and the Founders for not doing enough to extinguish a social system now universally reviled when we don't have to deal with the complex consequences of abolition. Slavery was woven into the cultural and economic fabric of American society, and it could not be so easily removed even by those who deeply hated it. Given this reality, it is perhaps less remarkable that they failed to immediately rid themselves of it, and more remarkable that their efforts put it on the inevitable path to extinction."[17]

When today's Americans condemn Jefferson for failing to free his slaves few realize the obstacles that confronted manumission in his era. Many Southern states had laws that did not permit slaves to be

---

17 Jerrett Stepman, *The War on History*, 84

set free unless their former masters left them in a condition in which they were unlikely to become destitute and, therefore, a burden on the state. Consistent with the nature of farming, many plantations were heavily in debt. As in the North, when debts went into default, creditors were permitted to seize assets and sell them to pay-off the debts. In the South, slaves were among such assets. To prevent a plantation owner from stripping his estate of slaves, Virginia passed a law in 1792 that gave creditors the power to seize even some freed slaves to satisfy debts. Often those creditors were ultimately Northern banks. Without such a law, owners with a fatal illness might have been more often tempted to free their slaves in their wills.

When he was 45 years old, six years before being elected President, Abraham Lincoln said, "When the Southern people tell us they are no more responsible for the origin of slavery, than we; I acknowledge the fact. When it is said that the institution exists; and that it is very difficult to get rid of it, in any satisfactory way, I can understand and appreciate the saying. I surely will not blame them for not doing what I should not know how to do myself."[18]

In recent decades Jefferson has been increasingly accused of fathering at least one child by a slave named Sally Hemmings. Until then most historians dismissed the arguments as stemming from the revengeful allegations of a disgruntled former Jefferson political supporter and journalist, James Callender. In 1998 DNA testing showed that at least one of Sally's children, Eston, shared genetic heritage with the Jefferson family. Yet the father remains unknown because there are over two dozen potential candidates for paternity.

Nevertheless, as cancel culture gained momentum the administrators at Jefferson's Monticello memorial tried to end the debate in 2018 by declaring Eston to be Thomas Jefferson's child. In truth, it is far from settled fact. Next, social justice historians added two-plus-two and got twenty-two by claiming that Sally was raped. Yet when Thomas Jefferson served as ambassador to France, he took Hemmings and a male slave to Paris with him. Even though slavery was illegal in France, Hemmings never petitioned for her freedom, as might be expected if Thomas had raped her. We can never know what

---

18 Abraham Lincoln, *Peoria Speech,* October 16, 1854: https://tinyurl.com/yc6zrjbj

truly happened, if anything, between Thomas Jefferson and Sally Hemmings, but that doesn't stop the allegation of a relationship being used as a handy club by Jefferson's detractors.

Finally, it should be noted that Jefferson was a key supporter of the 1787 Northwest Ordinance that prohibited slavery in the states formed out of the territories north of the Ohio River and east of the Mississippi River. It was passed under the Articles of Confederation two years before the adoption of our 1789 Constitution. Three years before the Ordinance, in 1784, Jefferson backed a bill that would have outlawed slavery in any state admitted after 1800. The bill failed by a single vote, which Jefferson claims would have been cast by fellow Virginian James Monroe had Monroe not been too ill to be present.[19]

The current focus on historical slavery has left one of Jefferson's most significant contributions almost unnoticed. Specifically, as a proponent of an agrarian economy he left a legacy of property ownership. When he became President in 1800 America had more property owners than did all of Europe even though the Old-World countries had thirty times the population. The statistic was a harbinger of the great property-holding middle class that would make America an economic powerhouse, even though not predominantly agrarian.

During his presidency he enlarged the opportunities for property ownership by acquiring the Louisiana Territory. Her frontier would become destinations for land-hungry European immigrants for more than a century. If not purchased by Jefferson, states in the region would have become the properties of French or Spanish monarchs. It is, therefore, ironic that the modern Louisiana state Democrat Party has minimized its connection to Jefferson. Without him the state would have become part of a European empire, before perhaps transitioning into an impoverished nation like Mexico.[20]

---

19 Jerrett Stepman, *The War on History*, 88-90

20 Jerrett Stepman, *The War on History*, 97

CONCLUSION

IN NOVEMBER 2021, Virginia voters firmly rejected Critical Race Theory. Well publicized mistreatment of parents at Loudoun County school board meetings while they voiced their concerns over the teaching of CRT and identity-based doctrines triggered the state's political realignment. Even though Democrat President Joe Biden won the state by ten percentage points only a year earlier, Virginia elected a Republican Governor based on the candidate's opinion that the state's school boards should treat parents respectfully and take their concerns seriously. The state also elected a Republican black female as Lieutenant Governor. Having been born in Jamaica and serving in the United States Marine Corps, she is proud to be an American. Like many of the Caribbean immigrant blacks that Ibram Kendi resents, she proudly admits that she is living proof of the American dream.

Many Americans outside of Virginia are also rejecting CRT and Identity Politics. At this writing federal, state, and local entities are acting. Among the federal actions is the Senate's proposed Stop CRT Act. It would withhold funding from schools and universities that promote CRT and similar race-based theories. Additionally, seven Senate Republicans introduced a bill in 2021, titled the Saving History Act, that would withhold federal funding, with some exceptions, from schools that teach the "1619 Project."

At the state level Texas passed a bill in September of 2021 that makes significant changes in the education of civics and establishes a new training program for teachers. It requires that both sides of controversial issues be presented and prohibits any academic credit for advocacy work. An Oklahoma law prohibits public schools from requiring students to participate in mandatory transgender and diversity training. It bans specified concepts of race and gender in public schools. Iowa bans the inclusion of stated concepts about race and sex into mandatory training for government employees, teachers, and students. Tennessee bans public and charter schools from teaching certain concepts about race and sex and withholds state funding for violations. Other bans have been implemented in Arizona, Idaho, New Hampshire, and South Carolina. The state school boards in Florida, Georgia, Utah, and Alabama introduced guidelines barring CRT-related discussions.[1]

Although CRT has been facing headwinds since the November 2021 elections, opponents must not relax their efforts. Many of the well-funded think tanks and charitable foundations are caught up in the vortex of the dreadful CRT and Identity Victimhood fraud. The Big Tech and Big Media companies also endorse it. Fortunately, truth and reality are against it. Eventually reality causes all mirages to vanish. Our job is to make them vanish while America still has a government worth saving.

THE END

---

1 Rashana Ray and Alexandra Gibbons, "Why are states banning CRT?," *Brookings Institution,* (November 2021): https://tinyurl.com/2p84m5f4

BIBLIOGRAPHY

U. S. Government

de Rugy, Veronique. "The Gender Gap, Paid Leave Programs and the Soviet Union," *Office of the Comptroller of Currency*, (October 18, 2021): https://tinyurl.com/2p9hkda6

Department of Defense, *Population Representation of the Military Services, Fiscal Year 2013*: https://tinyurl.com/2p9cn9ze

Military Leadership Diversity Commission, "From Representation to Inclusion: Diversity Leadership During the 21st Century," (March 15, 2011): https://tinyurl.com/yckkshh2

Books

Bradford, Gamaliel. *Lee the American,* (Cambridge: The Riverside Press, 1912).

Dattel, Gene. *Reckoning With Race*, (New York: Encounter Books, 2017).

Davis, William C. *The Cause Lost*, (Lawrence: Kansas University Press, 1996).

Delgado, Richard and Sefancic, Jean. *Critical Race Theory: Third Edition,* (New York, NYU Press, 2017).

Donald, David Herbert. *Lincoln,* (Jonathan Cape, London, 1995).

Dowdey, Clifford. *Lee,* (New York: Skyhorse Publishing, 2015).

—————————. *Lee's Last Campaign,* (New York: Skyhorse Publishing, 1999).

Eicher, David J. *The Longest Night,* (New York: Simon & Schuster, 2001).

Farrell, Warren. *The Myth of Male Power*, (New York: Simon and Schuster, 1993).

Farrell, Warren and Gray, John. *The Boy Crisis,* (Dallas: BenBella Books, 2019).

Freeman, Douglas Southall *R. E. Lee: Volume 4*, (New York: Charles Scribner & Sons, 1948).

Fremantle, Lt. Col. Arthur J. L. *Three Months in the Southern States,* (Lincoln: University of Nebraska Press, 1991).

Gallagher, Gary. *Lee and His Generals in War and Memory,* (Baton Rouge: Louisiana State University Press, 1998).

Hawley, Senator Josh *The Tyranny of Big Tech*, (Washington, D.C.: Regnery Publishing, 2021).

Horowitz, David. *The Enemy Within*, (Washington, D. C.: Regnery Publishing, 2021).

Johnson, Paul. *A History of the American People,* (New York, Harper Perennial, 1997).

Kendi, Ibram. *How to Be an Antiracist*, (New York, One World, 2019).

Levin, Mark. *American Marxism,* (New York, Threshold Editions, 2021).

Lohmeier, Lt. Col. Matthew. *Irresistible Revolution: Marxism's Goal of Conquest & The Unmaking of the American Military,* (Self Published, 2021).

MacDonald, Heather. *The War on Cops,* (New York: Encounter Books, 2016).

_____. *The Diversity Delusion,* (New York: St. Martin's Press, 2018).

Murray, Douglas. *The Madness of Crowds,* (London, Bloomsbury Continuum, 2019).

Nicolay, John and Hay, John. *Abraham Lincoln: A History, Volume 10,* (New York: Century Publishers, 1890).

Phillips, Robert. *Shelby Foote: Novelist and Historian,* (Jackson: University of Mississippi Press, 1992).

Steele, Shelby. *White Guilt,* (New York: Harper Perennial, 2006).

Stepman, Jerrett. *The War on History,* (Washington, D. C.: Regnery Publishing, 2019).

Thomas, Emory. *Robert E. Lee: A Biography* (New York: W. W. Norton, 1995).

Tucker, Glenn. *High Tide at Gettysburg,* (Gettysburg: Stan Clark Military Books, 1995).

Zinn, Howard. *A People's History of the United States,* (New York: HarperCollins, 1999).

NEWSPAPERS AND MAGAZINES

Abbot, Dorian and Marinovic, Ivan. "The Diversity Problem on Campus," *Newsweek,* (August 12, 2021).

Abcarian, Robin. "Mike Pence won't dine alone with a woman," *The Los Angeles Times,* (April 5, 2017): https://tinyurl.com/2p84e97r

Associated Press, "Zimmerman Alleged Police Brutality,"(May 24, 2012): https://tinyurl.com/dsw6cd77

Belkin, Douglas. "American Men Give Up On College, 'I Just Feel Lost,'" *The Wall Street Journal,* (September 6, 2021): https://tinyurl.com/2p9abxa3

Booth, Robert. "Sheryl Sandberg Calls for Policy Changes," *The Guardian,* (July 30, 2017): https://tinyurl.com/2p9yzeb7

Braswell, Sean. "Why the U.S. Military is so Southern," *OZY,* (November 19, 2016): https://tinyurl.com/ynjf32sp

Brown, Lee and Chamberlain, Samuel. "Kamala Harris Sidelined Amid Growing Tensions With Biden," *New York Post* (November 15, 2021): https://tinyurl.com/tcwjtjda

Coaston, Jane. "The Intersectionality Wars," *Vox,* May 28, 2019: https://tinyurl.com/bdhrtncm

Dean, Grace. "House antitrust report accuses Amazon of using third party seller data to copy popular products . . .," *Business Insider,* (October 7, 2020): https://tinyurl.com/2p8rpmu3

Dickstein, Corey. "Quite Intense: Public Offers 27,000 Suggestions. . .," *Stars and Stripes,* (October 1, 2021): https://tinyurl.com/2p966zw4

Draper, Kevin. "A Disparaging Video Prompts a Fallout at ESPN," *New York Times,* (July 4, 2021): https://tinyurl.com/222sscup

Dreher, Rod. "Professor: Intellectual Rigor is Racist," *The American Conservative,* (October 20, 2021).

Editorial Board, The. "One year later, *The Post's* Hunter Biden Reporting is Vindicated," *New York Post,* (October 12, 2021): https://tinyurl.com/bdh8m9kb

Free Press Journal, "Kamala Harris had an affair with a 60-year-old married man when she was 29,"(August 13, 2020): https://tinyurl.com/mr4aneu6

Gecker, Jocelyn. "Ethnic Studies Made High School Requirement," *Associated Press,* (October 8, 2021): https://tinyurl.com/53ypsaze

Grier, Peter. "Election Results 2012: Who Won it for Obama," *Christian Science Monitor,* (November 7, 2021): https://tinyurl.com/pz9jxy9r

Guynn, Jessica. "New California Law Requires Racial Diversity," *USA Today,* (September 30, 2020): https://tinyurl.com/bdd8kv2h

Hegarty, Noirin and Watt, Robert. "No Country for White Men . . .," *The Times (London),* (November 7, 2021): https://tinyurl.com/4jd8rs56

Horn, Sanford. "As Leftists Cry 'White Supremacy,' a Black Republican Makes History. . .," *The Federalist,* (November 4, 2021): https://tinyurl.com/h5dewjx2

Hudley, Cynthia "Achievement and Expectations of Immigrant, Second Generation and Non-Immigrant Black Student in U. S. Higher Education," *International Journal of Educational Psychology,* (October 24, 2016).

Johnson, Theodore. "A Missed Opportunity in Racial Preferences," *The Wall Street Journal,* (June 24, 2013.)

Joseph, B. "Why Nigerian Americans are One of the Most Successful Ethnic Groups in the U.S.," *Medium,* (July 2, 2018): https://tinyurl.com/yc5ejse4

Kuhn, David. "Exit Polls: How Obama Won," *Politico,* (November 5, 2008): https://tinyurl.com/bddc7epn

Lajka, Arijeta. "Robert E. Lee Owned Slaves," *Associated Press,* (June 12, 2020): https://tinyurl.com/ms47hr6

Leigh, Philip. "Six Reasons to Leave Andrew Jackson on the $20 bill," *The Hill,* (September 26, 2019); https://tinyurl.com/2p8h6hp8

Melley, Brian. "California Law Says Corporate Boards Need Women. Is it legal?," *Associated Press* (December 1, 2021): https://tinyurl.com/2p85decf

Ngo, Andy. "Men Behind the Conceptual Penis Hoax . . .," *The College Fix,* (May 22, 2017): https://tinyurl.com/2p96e82t

Perez-Pena, Richard. "1 in 4 Women Experience Sexual Assault on Campus," *The New York Times,* (September 21, 2015): https://tinyurl.com/3ka8txf3

Ponnuru, Ramesh. "Stop Lauding General Milley's Evasions on CRT," *Bloomberg,* (June 29, 2021): https://tinyurl.com/yckm2arm

Prince, Zenitha "Higher Percentage of Black Children Live With Single Mothers," *Afro News,* December 31, 2016: https://tinyurl.com/2p833cam

Robin, Corey. "Clarence Thomas's Radical Vision of Race," *The New Yorker,* (September 19, 2019).

Rufo, Christopher. "Liberals were losing the argument over critical race theory in schools—Time to Call in the FBI," *New York Post,* (October 6, 2021).

——————————. "Christopher Rufo on Woke Capital," *City Journal,* (October 28, 2021) https://www.city-journal.org/christopher-rufo-on-woke-capital

Rosales, John and Walker, Tim. "The Racist Beginnings of Standardized Testing," *neaNow,* (March 20, 2012): https://tinyurl.com/yc3e8fe2

Salzman, Philip. "False Justification for Anti-Racism," *Epoch Times,* (September 8, 2021).

Soave, Robby. "Anti-PC Writers Trick Seven Academic Journals into Accepting Hoax Papers. . .," *Reason,* (October 3, 2018): https://tinyurl.com/329fp45b

Steel, Emily and Schmidt, Michael. "Bill O'Reilly Settled New Harassment Claim . . .," *The New York Times,* (October 21, 2017): https://tinyurl.com/y75rn9dn

Thompson, Derek. "Colleges Have a Guy Problem," *The Atlantic,* (September 14, 2021): https://tinyurl.com/eb4ehay4

Vakil, Caroline. "Republicans Press Milley . . .," *The Hill,* (November 4, 2021): https://tinyurl.com/4sd49unj

Ward, Alex. "The Pentagon is Taking a Major Step to Deal with Diversity," *Vox,* (February 12, 2021): https://tinyurl.com/2p84xyh8

Wirth, Lewis. "Education for Survival: The Jews," *American Journal of Sociology,* V. 48, N. 6 (May, 1943).

Zinn, Howard. "Making History," *New York Times: Letter to Editor,* (July 1, 2007): https://tinyurl.com/2p9638wt

RESEARCH PAPERS AND SURVEYS

Akerlof, George and Yellen, Janet. "An Analysis of Out of Wedlock Births in the United States," *Brookings Institute,* (August 1, 1996): https://tinyurl.com/49c77dsx

Amos, Jason. "Young Black Men Without High School Diplomas," *Pew Research,* (October 10, 2010): https://tinyurl.com/3ffykxbm

Butcher, Jonathan and Gonzalez, Mike. "Critical Race Theory, the New Intolerance, and It's Grip on America," *Heritage Foundation,* (December 7, 2020).

Butcher, Jonathan. "The *New York Times* Has Started Correcting the Historical Record in the '1619 Project'," *Heritage Foundation,* (May 16, 2020): https://tinyurl.com/vzk8rbdz;

Clegg, Roger. "Percentage of Births to Unmarried Women," *Center for Equal Opportunity.* (February 26, 2020): https://tinyurl.com/mvmwnhrd

Horowitz, Juliana, Brown, Anna, Cox, Kiana. "The Role of Race and Ethnicity in Americans' Personal Lives," *Pew Research Center,* (April 9, 2019): https://tinyurl.com/yw8h5xed

McLaughlin, Jim and Schmidt, Rob. "National Undergraduate Study: Executive Summary," *McLaughlin & Associates,* 6-7, (September 28, 2021).

National Center for Educational Statistics: https://tinyurl.com/5aty5r56

Perry, Mark. "Bulk of Earnings Gender Gap Can be Explained ...," *Foundation for Economic Education,* (September 6, 2021): https://tinyurl.com/9hbykxd8

Ray, Rashana and Gibbons, Alexandra. "Why are states banning CRT?," *Brookings Institution,* (November 2021): https://tinyurl.com/2p84m5f4

Sommers, Christina Hoff. "The Gender Wage Gap Myth," *American Enterprise Institute,* (February 3, 2014): https://tinyurl.com/yc2b9pah

INTERVIEWS

Loury, Glenn. *Hoover Institution Interview*, (November 22, 2021): https://tinyurl.com/mr2t5scv

WEBSITES

Black Demographics, "Households,": https://tinyurl.com/ms228h4f

Bowman, Tom "The Military Confronts Extremism," *NPR*, (April 7, 2021): https://tinyurl.com/7vffz36f

College Factual, Yale University: Student Racial-Ethnic Demographics: https://tinyurl.com/2p996x5s

Cruz, Senator Ted "Critical Race Theory," *Leadership Institute,* (November 2021): https://tinyurl.com/f3tcyx2w;

Dougherty, Michael. "NBC: We're Sorry We Edited the Trayvon Martin Tape . . .," *NBC* (April 4, 2012): https://tinyurl.com/2p82z2ts

Ghosh, Iman "Visualizing Population by Race," *Visual Capitalist,* (December 28, 2020): https://tinyurl.com/nyrj5tr7

Kendi, Ibram. "Pass an Anti-Racist Constitutional Amendment," *Politico*: https://tinyurl.com/3dmk5ajw

Kurtzleben, Danielle."Top General Defends Studying CRT," *NPR*, (June 23, 2021): https://tinyurl.com/mt3n2fra

Levy, Ari. "The most liberal and conservative tech companies ranked by employees' political donations," *CNBC,* (July 2, 2020): https://tinyurl.com/59erjv8j

Liu, Grace. "Why Tiger Moms are Great," *CNN,* (May 17, 2013): https://tinyurl.com/2p9hdbvr

Lincoln, Abraham. *Peoria Speech,* October 16, 1854: https://tinyurl.com/yc6zrjbj

Lusane, Clarance. "Whitewashing Our First President," *Zinn Education Project*: https://tinyurl.com/2p99p2cm

National Healthy Marriage Resource Center, "Asian & Pacific Islander,": https://tinyurl.com/yc6cb5h5

Post Millennial "Woke U.S. Navy Names Ship After Accused pedophile, Harvey Milk," (November 8, 2021): https://tinyurl.com/2p89eyu9

Tobak, Steve. "The Gender Pay Gap is a Complete Myth," *CBS,* (April 17, 2011): https://tinyurl.com/yckhnytx

UCLA Microaggression List (2014): https://tinyurl.com/2p94mkyv

Waltz, Michael (Congressman). "Waltz Presses Austin on CRT," Press Release, (June 23, 2021): https://tinyurl.com/mrxzt48x

_____. "Waltz Requests Critical Race Theory Materials from West Point," Press Release, (April 8, 2021): https://tinyurl.com/46tjv4ra

Wikipedia, "Son Preference in China,": https://tinyurl.com/2p8698pw

_____. Jaime Escalante, https://en.wikipedia.org/wiki/Jaime_Escalante

_____. "George Michael Zimmerman," https://en.wikipedia.org/wiki/George_Zimmerman

Yale University, Hillel Guide: https://tinyurl.com/bddb84ma

Other Books By Philip Leigh

The Devil's Town

U. S. Grant's Failed Presidency

Causes of the Civil War

Trading With the Enemy

Lee's Lost Dispatch and Other Civil War Controversies

Co. Aytch: Illustrated and Annotated

Southern Reconstruction

The Confederacy at Flood Tide

Florida's Cattle Wars

Made in the USA
Columbia, SC
03 March 2022

56758155R00068